AS I RECALL IT

AS I RECALL IT

Living Beneath the
Wings of Angels

BILLY ROBERTS

APEX PUBLISHING LTD

First published in 2009 by
Apex Publishing Ltd
PO Box 7086, Clacton on Sea, Essex, CO15 5WN

www.apexpublishing.co.uk

British Library Cataloguing-in-Publication Data
A catalogue record for this book
is available from the British Library

ISBN 1-906358-50-8   978-1-906358-50-1

Typeset in 11pt Baskerville Win95 BT

Production Manager: Chris Cowlin

Cover Design: Siobhan Smith

Printed by the MPG Books Group in the UK

Authors Dedication
I dedicate this book to my wife Dolly, for all her love and support

FOREWORD

The world of the paranormal is saturated with claimants, those people who profess to have a special ability. Whether that ability is divining information from a personal item, or communing with departed loved ones, or even pointing out your current mood from the colour of your aura, all special claimants have a story to tell. And, boy, are there a lot of stories. When my interest in this field began as a teenager I was voraciously reading every story-filled psychic autobiography I could lay my hands on. Initially I read the stories by Estelle Roberts, Rita Rogers, Doris Stokes and Uri Geller but as the years progressed new claimants rose up through the ranks: Gordon Smith, John Edward, James Van Praagh, Sylvia Browne, Colin Fry, Tony Stockwell and even Derek Acorah. I found all these life stories absolutely fascinating. I became swept away by the convoluted rationale for an alleged ability, the insight into a family that, more often than not, showed a heritage of psychic ability whilst occasionally hinting at disdain elsewhere in the family tree. I marvelled at the often misinterpreted childhood personal experience (at least in my opinion) that, in hindsight, was the first indication that "I was different". I was enthralled by the brief foray into an alternative career in which there was always the thought that something else was drawing them onto another path. I also smirked at the detail recounted in successful readings and the glowing testimonials and life-changing effect an encounter with this special claimant would have.

In picking up Billy's autobiography I expected no less, and I wasn't disappointed but also I was pleasantly surprised. Here we have a life story that begins with childhood confrontations with the medical profession and the influential figure Annie (both Billy's mother and a life-changing meeting at age 2). We have various colourful characters from the family who either accept and support or become intriguing skeletons stepping out of the closet. We even have the archetypal retelling of an encounter with spirits, an encounter which becomes highly accurate when confirmed by a flamboyant "parapsychologist". But here, instead of the usual settings found in psychic biographies, we are treated to an adventure in a graveyard deep in the Louisiana swamps, and the symbolic appearance of a white owl!

It is occasional nuggets of excitement like this that pepper the background and give a context that really makes this autobiography stand out. It would be so easy to get bogged down in psychic re-telling and evidence for yet another ability, but Billy doesn't. We have a story here which takes us on a vivid journey through the 1950s, 60s, and on to present day. A journey which is littered with passing references to key historical figures, culture and places: Bert Weedon, Dick Barton (Special Agent), Frankie Vaughan, Penny Lane, Mick Jagger, The Yardbirds, The Locomotive Club, Chuck Berry, Jimi Hendrix, Dunkirk, Ken Dodd, Doris Stokes, Screaming Lord Sutch, Big Breakfast, Russell Grant, etc, etc, etc. For Billy is a rare commodity – an unhealthy child who doctors insisted wouldn't live, a 1960s music career in which he really lived the decade, and survived. So these are no mere passing references that I list above, often they are personal encounters that enthral and sometimes amuse.

So whether you are fascinated by the spirit encounters of a psychic and medium, or whether you love hearing treasured anecdotes of encounters with equally colourful characters, this is the story for you. As Billy recalls it, your reading eyes widen first in disbelief but then in gratitude at being immersed in the retelling of a colourful past, present and, as Billy would have it, future.

Dr. Ciarán O'Keeffe

vi

INTRODUCTION

Having been psychic since I was a child, it is really very difficult for me to know what it's like not to be psychic. In fact, seeing so-called 'dead' people was commonplace to me growing up in Liverpool, and it wasn't until I was around the age of nine or ten that I realised that not all children were the same as me. Looking back on my life, I can now see that being psychic from so young an age really did have a profound effect upon me, both psychologically and emotionally, and really was responsible for many of the deep insecurities that constantly trouble me today. For a good part of my childhood I lived in a veritable world of fantasy and imagination, and always felt 'different' from other children who never really knew what to make of me. At the age of three I contracted whooping cough, which in turn left me with an incurable respiratory disease diagnosed as bilateral basal Bronchiectasis, and as a direct result of this I spent most of each year either in Alder Hey Hospital, or tucked up in bed at home. This, in itself, meant that I was never involved in rough-and-tumble games, and also alienated me from other children. Although I did have some very good friends, I spent most of my childhood by myself, and was frequently left to my own devices and forced to amuse myself. This meant that I was quite introverted and had lots of time to focus my attention on my many spirit visitors, which to me were as solid and tangible as any living person. I suppose I was made to feel different, and although my parents had been told in no uncertain terms, not to expect me to live to see my teens, I always knew that I wasn't going to die, and that I had something very important to do in life. This may sound a little pretentious, but I can't describe it in any other way. From as early as six years old I became extremely religious, and although my parents were not, I prayed every night before I went to sleep. There was little surprise then that I wanted to be a priest, and really believed that my visions were in fact a gift from God. Somewhere around the age of fourteen, my headmaster, Mr Mcmennamin, disabused me of this notion, and said, 'I have never heard anything more preposterous!' Then to add insult to injury he informed me that, besides not being a Catholic, I would never meet the academic requirements necessary to enter the seminary. I never forgave him for that, but in later life secretly thanked him for the cold awakening.

Preparing for all eventualities, just in case I did survive my school leaving days, my parents encouraged my interest in music. 'At least then he will have some sort of a career!' said my father, thinking ahead as he always did. 'Who knows, he might even become famous.' Although he never really believed that for one moment, he did have it all planned. It was some time around 1954, I was eight, and my big brother, Alby's friend, Georgie Hill, had bought a Hofner guitar from one of the main music stores in the Liverpool City Centre, and had invited me round to see it. It was love at first sight, and from then on I knew that all I wanted to do was play the guitar in a Rock 'n Roll group. Unable to afford a guitar, my mother bought me a ukulele instead, and although this only had four strings, opposed to a guitar's six, I mastered it within a few weeks. I spent the following twelve months busking outside the local pubs, and would return home with my pockets full of pennies. My brother, Alby, eventually bought me my very first guitar for Christmas, and then as far as I was concerned my future as a Rock star was already becoming a reality. I played my guitar all the time, and even took it with me to bed. Although it was quite obvious to my parents that I did have an aptitude for the guitar, without some form of tuition, I was limited to what I could do. At this point an elderly neighbour, George Edwards, stepped into the rescue. He had played the guitar in a Big Band during World War Two, and with a little persuasion from my mother he agreed to teach me. His lessons consisted of a few chords scribbled on the inside of a Woodbine cigarette packet. However, he underestimated my enthusiasm, and when I began knocking on his front door several times a day for more chords, he decided that, due to other commitments he no longer had the time. Drastic measures were called for! The legendary guitarist Bert Weedon had just published a book entitled: 'PLAY IN A DAY.' My mother bought me the book and I wrote to him at the address given on the back of cover. To my parent's surprise I received a letter from him personally written. He even scribbled a few chords for me on the back of his letter. As if that wasn't enough; I used to receive a letter from him every couple of months or so, asking how my guitar playing was coming along, and keeping me updated about his new releases. I've still got a signed photograph he sent to me, and he recently replied to an email I sent him. He even said he remembered writing to me.

It never occurred to me that I would one day use my psychic and mediumistic skills as a profession. Of course, in the 1950s and 60s mediums were not seen on stage or television, and I just accepted my psychic experiences as an integral part of who I was. I wanted so much to be a guitarist in a band, be famous and travel the world - so different from what I am doing today. I now know that my psychic skills were still there during my very exciting sojourn in the world of music, and that they were somehow channelled into the creative areas of my life. Although I have at times hit rock bottom during my life, I can honestly say that I would not have changed one single thing.

Since my first autobiography, Beneath The Wings of Angels was published in 1995, my work as a medium has changed remarkably. I no longer serve Spiritualist Churches, which meant traipsing up and down the country in hail, rain or snow often without so much a 'thank you' or even a cup of tea. I have appeared on television all over the world, visited a haunted graveyard deep within the Louisiana swamps, been thrown against a wall by a poltergeist in a Victorian house, and presented a series of videos entitled BILLY ROBERTS INVESTIGATES THE PARANORMAL. On which I was seen visiting haunted locations all over the north west of England, (long before the popular television programme, Most Haunted.) I have also co-written a book with Dr Ciaran O'Keeffe, (of Most Haunted fame,) entitled THE GREAT PARANORMAL CLASH, published in July 2008. Apart from all this today I try to lead a comparatively quiet life writing, and in July 2008 The Trinity Mirror Group published my first children's book, THE MAGIC LOCKER. I have also turned this into a children's musical theatre production, to be staged for one week at The Liverpool Empire, beginning on 14th September 2009, for which I have written all the music. So, I am sure you will agree, my work as a medium has changed considerably over the last 10 years.

While I was appearing on a radio programme a few years ago, I was asked if I regret any part of my life. I can honestly say that if I had my life over again, I most probably would not change one thing. My mentor, Tall Pine once said to me, 'you are who you are today as a direct result of who you were yesterday.' And I do believe this to be true. The Law of Karma is in constant operation all through our lives. And although theology teaches that we are punished for our sins, the higher teachings tell us in no uncertain terms that, 'we are not punished for our sins - we are punished by our own ignorance – by our own mistakes.' This said, I do wonder whether I'll ever work through my own Karma, as it seems to be a never-ending cycle.

CHAPTER ONE
MY CHILDHOOD

My entrance into this world on June 24th 1946 was most probably not the momentous occasion my mother always led me to believe it was, but nonetheless, for me personally it was the very beginning of an extremely unusual and very exciting life, and one I don't think I would have changed in any way whatsoever. In fact, the morning of the day my mother went into labour, she found an old, and very bent crucifix on the step, and immediately took that to be some sort of a 'sign' about the child to which she was shortly to give birth. I'm quite sure that when my mother saw exactly what I was like once I had reached my teens, she knew then that the whole symbology of the bent cross was certainly portentous of something. My father, Albert, frequently looked at me and mumbled, 'I don't know what's going to become of you, lad!' And although when I was in my early teens I would cynically dismiss his words, today I am beginning to realise that my father must have had some sort of insight into my future, as I now fully agree with him: 'What is going to become of me?'

When I was born my parents, Annie and Albert Roberts already had a ten-year-old son, also called Albert, or Alby as he was and still is affectionately known. Whilst my mother was giving birth to me in Sefton General Hospital, Smithdown Road in Wavertree, (a district in Liverpool,) my mother's sister, aunty Sadie, took my brother to the Astoria Cinema in Anfield. And so, at 6.50pm on Monday 24th June 1946, William Henry Roberts, or 'Billy' as I became known, was born.

I was christened at St Bridget's Church in Bagot Street,

Wavertree and, according to my mother, the proudest day of my father's life. My God parents were aunty Sadie and Archie Green, a scrap dealer friend of my fathers. Archie Green was apparently a heavy drinker and someone who ended his life as a derelict. I thought Godparents were supposed to set an example and give spiritual guidance! This has always confused me. However, aunty Sadie fulfilled her position perfectly, and in fact cared for me right up until the day she died in 1998.

When I was born, my parents Annie and Albert lived at 30 Grosvenor Road, Wavertree in Liverpool, in a three up and two down terraced house with a back yard and outside toilet. Wavertree had always been a close-knit community, with ever-open front doors down every street. Its streets were quite narrow, some of them cobbled, and the small terrace houses had front doors, which opened directly onto the street. They all had two rooms downstairs; the front parlour, which looked out onto the street, and the back room, which occasionally doubled as a kitchen and family room. Upstairs there were two bedrooms and one very small 'box room' as it was called. All the houses had small backyards, separated from each other by high walls. The back-yard door opened onto a communal, cobbled entry. Because there was no bathroom in our house, bath nights for me as a child meant sitting in a tin bath in front of a roaring coal fire, listening to Life with the Lyons or Dick Barton Special Agent, on the crackly wireless that stood on the shelf in the corner of the room. In the early fifties television was in its innovative stages and so the wireless, as it was then called, was the main source of family entertainment. The inhabitants of Wavertree had suffered greatly through the war together, helping each other in as many ways as possible. The community spirit had never wavered, and although you may look hard to find it today, when I was born in 1946 it was still very much in evidence. Front doors were open most of the day and

2

neighbours were often seen gossiping in small groups on the doorsteps or gathering in someone's parlour for tea. Everyone knew everyone else's business and my mother, Annie Roberts, knew more than most – but if you wanted someone to keep a secret then Annie Roberts was the woman to speak to. Neighbours constantly sought her out for help and advice. She was a steady, dependable woman, immensely strong physically and emotionally, and whose presence in a crisis always inspired confidence. In fact, she always had an answer; she always seemed to know what to do and how to do it. She was frequently called upon to help with situations ranging from childbirth (and she delivered more than one with her own hands), to violent arguments between neighbours. She was an excellent seamstress too and made clothes for most of the neighbours and family, which was an added benefit, as she had very little money and couldn't afford to buy them. Money was usually short and my mother was no stranger to scrimping and saving to make ends meet. Although my father allegedly had money, he was quite miserly and always complained that 'Times had been hard, and money was scarce'. As he came from a fairly wealthy family this was far from the truth. He did have money and he knew exactly what to do with it. Unlike today, we were the only family in the street with a telephone and a car, and the neighbours always looked upon my father as someone who was successful and fairly well off. Whenever my mother was faced with any sort of a crisis, she would simply push her shiny black hair back off her forehead, take a deep breath and tackle the job. Although my father was quite volatile, it was obvious to everyone that my mother wore the trousers, and my father would not make any major decisions without having approval from my mother.

My father, Albert Roberts, was a self-employed general dealer and dismantler. He had a finger in many pies – buying, selling and renovating just about everything. One

3

month the house and backyard would be full of old washing machines which he and my mother would renovate, paint and then sell, and the next month engine parts and even complete engines would be piled up one on top of the other in the hallway, backyard and living room, playing havoc on everyone's shins. On one occasion I remember my father returning from the auction room with a van full of stuff he had bought. My mother was cooking the evening meal when he announced that he had bought some silk material, which she could probably use to make some blouses and other items of clothing to sell. After excitedly rummaging through the boxes in the back of the van, my mother found some brass handles on top of the silk fabric. After closely examining them she realised that they were coffin handles, and the silk material was a collection of shrouds. My father then admitted that he had bought an undertaker's entire bankruptcy stock, and then joked that five top of the range coffins were being delivered the following day. Needless to say my mother's protestations could be heard all over the street, and so he sold the entire stock to his friend, Tommy Oldham. Anything for a quiet life, that was my dad.

When I was three years old I contracted whooping cough and was admitted to Woolton, Baby Hospital's specialist unit, where it was found that I had bilateral basal Bronchiectasis, dilation of the bronchial tubes. This is a debilitating respiratory disease, and although not many sufferers are found today, it does accompany the symptoms of cystic fibrosis. In the late forties this condition was virtually untreatable, and also meant that I produced copious amounts of sputum, often blood-stained. I had to be subjected to the very tiring, daily process of 'postural drainage,' a procedure in which my back would have to be repeatedly pounded whilst I was lying face down in a horizontal position. To keep my lungs free of infection, physiotherapy had to be applied several times a day, (and still is today, although I manage it differently.) This meant that as a result of the disease I spent many months of the year either in hospital, or in bed at home. I was kept in Woolton Baby Hospital (no longer there,) for 12 months, before being sent home. From then on I was transferred to Alder Hey Children's Hospital in Liverpool, to where I was admitted two or three times a year for treatment. Because my disease was quite extensive, when I was four years old my parents were told in no uncertain terms, that as far as their prognosis was concerned I would not reach my teens. My future looked bleak, and my parents were prepared for the worse!

As antibiotics were in their innovative stages, treatment was limited and, as a consequence, I suffered with frequent bouts of pneumonia. Looking back I can see now that I really was quite pitiful. I do have to admit I was molly-coddled and spoilt. My circumstances meant that I was deprived of the company of other children, and as a result was forced to spend an awful lot of time alone. There is little wonder then that I became insecure and very introverted. As far as I can recall my psychic experiences began sometime around the age of three. Seeing so-called 'dead' people became commonplace to me, and although not all my experiences were pleasant, I did tend to think that it was quite normal and that everyone could see what I could see.

I was very close to my big brother Alby, and because he was ten years older than me he was protective towards me and looked after me in everyway possible. I suppose he was only too aware of the dark cloud that hovered above me and, like my parents, fully realised that I might not be around for very much longer. He was always bringing something home for me, and would frequently spend his pocket money on toys for me. I can remember Alby coming home from school one blustery day, clutching a brightly coloured, wooden parrot that he'd made for me in his woodwork class. I was four years old, and my mother had just finished securing the lino on the living room floor, and had left the hammer on the chair. Alby was teasing me by hiding the wooden parrot he had brought home for me, and seemed to delight in watching me throw a tantrum. He was sitting cross-legged on the floor, and when he wasn't looking, I picked up the hammer in both hands and whacked him over the head. Needless to say, his work of art was immediately thrown onto the back of the fire, and although he didn't require stitches, he did have a huge cut on his head, and a lump that lasted for weeks. I don't think he ever forgave me for that!

Although as a child I was totally unaware of the severity of my health, I did have a happy childhood and felt loved. Even between the ages of three and four I felt somehow different, and seeing so-called 'dead' people was quite normal for me. Although I must say, at that very young age I had no idea that the things I frequently saw were the apparitions of dead people.

I suppose my very first paranormal experience took place sometime between the ages of two and three. Annie Hurst was the 96-year-old next-door neighbour, an extremely kind old lady who would just walk in through our ever-open front door, just to take a look at me asleep in my pram. Annie Hurst had a very kind but lined face, and she always wore a red woollen shawl draped over her head and shoulders. 'My love!' she would say, leaning over the pram and smiling at me. 'My love!' Then, one sunny afternoon I was playing on the rug in front of the coal fire, when my mother picked me up and carried me to the front door. There were black limousines lined up outside, and people dressed in black climbing into them. 'Annie Hurst has gone to heaven!' my mother tried to explain. 'She won't be coming to see us any more!' I can recall looking at my mother, puzzled. Nothing of what she was saying made sense to me. I could see Annie Hurst standing there watching the sad faces climbing into the cars. She looked at me and smiled. 'My love!' she said. 'My love!' Of course, nobody else could see her!

Even at that young age I knew that Annie Hurst was not dead! In fact, to any child death is completely alien and simply does not make any sense. Some days after Annie Hurst's funeral I was playing on the rug in front of the fire, when the living room door opened by itself and I said 'Come in Annie Hurst.' My parents looked at me with amazement and then both swung their heads round to look at the door. Of course, only I knew that Annie Hurst had come to see me. This happened right up until I was about ten years old. My father tried everything to secure the living room door, but it would still swing open, 'Come in Annie Hurst,' I would always say. Then, without any warning whatsoever, Annie Hurst's entry into the living room ceased forever. I then knew that the kind old lady had gone home, and would not be calling to see me anymore.

Strange phenomena frequently occurred in our small terraced house in Grosvenor Road. As a young boy, when I was feeling sad, I would occasionally retreat to the stairs, where I would sit on the landing. With all the bedroom doors closed, I somehow felt safe and faraway from my troubles and worries. I suppose this was my sacred space, and a place in the world where nobody could touch me. It was quite dark there, and the sound echoed, and I used to imagine it was just like being in an underground cavern, somewhere faraway. Because it was so dark at the top of the stairs, I would occasionally see another little boy standing on the landing, just watching me as I sat alone. I was never afraid of him, and knew that he was feeling the same as me, lonely and sad. His name was David, and although he always kept his distance, I knew he wanted to sit with me. There would be the odd occasion when he would beat me to my sacred place, and I would see him sitting there at the top of the stairs, grinning mischievously at me. I never did find out who he was exactly, and wonder if he was just a reflection of me! To be quite honest, whenever I called to see my mother, I occasionally sat at the top of the stairs if I needed some peace and quiet and time to think, just as I did as a child. Needless to say, I never saw little David again. Maybe I am right and he was a reflection of me. I always referred to him as 'The Shadow On The Stairs!' In fact, my life has been peppered with shadows, of one kind or another; shadows of the past, and now shadows of the future!

CHAPTER TWO
THE EARLY YEARS

Sometime around the age of three I became acquainted with Tall Pine, a spirit, Native American Indian, or so I then thought, as later on in my life I discovered that he was far more. This will be explained further on in the book. Although today Spirit Guides are frequently the subject of jokes, Tall Pine, or TP as he is affectionately known, is a Spirit Guide and my mentor, and someone who watches over me. To me he appears as solid and tangible as any living person, and although he never seems to smile, he radiates a comforting warmth that reassures me. As a baby, to help me sleep, my mother would apparently attach a branch from a tree to the end of my pram, rather like a baby's mobile, and the sound of the leaves would lull me to sleep. I am quite sure now that the effect this had on me was something to do with Tall Pine who, one day, just appeared at the foot of my cot. As far as I can recall, TP never, ever spoke to me, although some form of dialogue – probably telepathic – did transpire between us. I would see his tall, shadowy silhouette at the foot of my cot, and would then fall asleep. Although today I do not always see TP, I am always aware of his presence, particularly when I need help.

Although my childhood was peppered with all different kinds of paranormal goings on, I did not walk about wearing a badge saying 'I AM PSYCHIC!' as many people today believe that I should have done. As far as those around me were concerned I was just 'different', and amongst my childhood friends there were perhaps only two who were aware of my strange and very unusual abilities. Apart from this, I suppose I was just like any other child my age, with one obvious difference: I was not allowed to get involved in rough and tumble games, or to play in the snow or rain, for fear that I would come down with pneumonia. I have only mentioned this, because people who knew me when I was in my teens today often make the crass comment, 'I don't remember you being psychic!' Some members of my family are also guilty of this unintelligent remark!

As there was plenty to do, for me growing up in the mid fifties was quite exciting. War-torn Liverpool had still not recovered from the battering of the Blitz, and so where I lived in Wavertree was a veritable adventure playground, with disused air-raid shelters everywhere, and even an ammunition dump under the 'Fairy Bridge' in Sefton Park. Although I never actually went into the War-refuse dump, I did use to keep watch whilst my friends invaded it, only to emerge with all sorts of interesting military artefacts, from dummy hand grenades, to bullets and even whole machine-gun magazines.

I started at Lawrence Road Infant School with my friend, Roger Gregeen, when I was five. Unlike me, Roger could already read and write and, as a result of his parents' pre-school tuition, was quite brainy. Roger used to help me a lot and would let me copy the answers to the sums that just went right over my head. To be quite honest I never could apply myself sufficiently, and so was always behind with my school work. Miss Jones was my first teacher and took me under her very maternal wing and looked after me. Even to this day, I am not sure whether being psychic made me insecure, or whether it was all the result of my debilitating illness. Apart from my frequent admissions to Alder Hey Hospital, I somehow managed to reach my seventh birthday, and the best birthday of my life. The summer of 1953 was extremely hot, and on the day of my birthday I had been with my friends to Wavertree Park, or the 'Mystery' as it is known. As soon as I set foot through the front door my big brother, Alby took me up to his room to give me my birthday present, my very first cricket set, a bat, wickets, a ball and shin pads. I couldn't believe it, and to this day I have never forgotten it.

When the school summer holidays had come to an end, to my dismay, I was transferred from Lawrence Road School to Sefton Park Junior School – the big boys school. It was then that growing up became a reality. Although a lot of my friends also attended Sefton Park School, the lads there were a lot rougher and more boisterous, and so I was forced to fend for myself. Even in those days bullying was quite prevalent, and the weakest were always targeted. I hated it, and even when there was nothing wrong with me I would pretend that I wasn't well so my mother would keep me off school. On one particular occasion I was waiting to go into The Ear Nose and Throat Hospital to have some abscesses removed from my ears. Although I wasn't feeling particularly well, my mother persuaded me to finish the weak off. My teacher was a young woman by the name of Miss Waddington. As far as I remember she seemed to always be angry and never smiled. She was talking to the class and could see that I was daydreaming (as I frequently did), and bellowed my name across the room. I was only vaguely aware that she was calling me and still did not take any notice. The next thing I knew she had smacked me across my ear, and the pain was so bad that I fainted. When I came to blood was oozing from my ear and the pain was unbearable. Another teacher took me home in his car and tried to no avail to pacify my mother. She immediately decided to take matters into her own hands, and demanded to be taken back to the school, her rage causing a look of total fear to show on the teacher's face. Holding on tightly to my hand, she stormed into the classroom and smacked Miss Waddington so hard that she fell against the blackboard. 'You'll never see my son again, and I hope that teaches you a lesson!' Today, of course, my mother could have sued the school, but in the fifties things were so different; parents frequently dealt with the matter themselves. That was my mother! She was not afraid of anything or anybody.

It was clear to everyone that I was far too frail to attend an ordinary school, and so on the recommendation of the consultant at Alder Hey Children's Hospital, a place was secured for me at Underlea Open Air School, a special school for children with chronic respiratory and breathing disorders. This was a fantastic school, and most certainly not like a school at all. Underlea Open Air School was situated in Aigburth in the suburbs of Liverpool, and was an old yellow-bricked mansion, in Baroque style architecture, set in eight acres of parkland and geometrically landscaped gardens. The old house had been built in 1859 by Charles Forget, a rich merchant who then sold it to another wealthy merchant by the name of Thomas Carlisle. The old mansion was then called Floraire, and before Thomas Carlisle died only three years later, he changed its name to Underlea, a name that remained with it until it was demolished in 1980. Although when I attended the school we were told that the Swiss consul donated the mansion to be used for the frail children of Liverpool, other reports say it was millionaire merchant, Hamilton Gilmour and his wife who actually donated it to the Liverpool Education Committee to be used for children with respiratory problems. It was a magnificent old house, and being there meant that we could be absent from school without having a visit from the school board and threatened with prosecution.

Even at school I was different and would frequently see things other children could not see.

MY FRIEND CAME TO SAY GOODBYE
At the age of nine my friend at Underlea was Terrence Davies. He was always getting into trouble, and although he bullied and terrorised the other kids, Terry was extremely

protective towards me. Although he looked fairly healthy in comparison to other children at the school, I had a strong feeling that he was in fact quite poorly. We'd just started school after the Christmas holidays and I was looking forward to seeing Terry again. He wasn't there and the teacher told me that my friend wasn't too well. In fact, he was off school for three weeks, and when he came back on the Monday morning I made a dash to greet him but something stopped me in my tracks. Terry was surrounded by a very dark grey cloud, and was ashen faced and seemed distant, just like a stranger. He never came near me all that day, and the following morning at assembly, the headmaster announced that Terrence Davies had passed away on the Sunday night, the night before I had seen him at school. It never dawned on me at all why nobody else had mentioned seeing him on the Monday at school. What I couldn't understand was why he seemed distant like a stranger, and not like my friend at all. My mother suggested that he had just come to say goodbye.

THE LADY OF LIGHT
What I have always referred to as my very first mystical experience took place when I was around nine years old, and this event was most definitely a catalyst where my spiritual development was concerned. Having a big brother, and someone to look up to, was always quite important to me when I was a child. As my brother was ten years older than me, I loved and admired him and wanted to be with him all the time. However, as Alby was growing up, he became more and more reluctant to look after his baby brother, and began to use every excuse not to look after me. By then Alby had met and fallen in love with Ethel Baxter, a woman who was a few years his senior. She lived with her family at 17a Lawrence Road, (parallel to Grosvenor Road,) above a butcher's shop. For reasons best known to my mother she

opposed the relationship. I suppose my father just went along with my mother, and Alby was warned, in no uncertain terms: 'If you don't finish with her you can get out of this house!' There was an awful row between my father and brother and, as a consequence, my brother packed his clothes and left! Both my mother and I were devastated, and my dad was in a fit of rage all that night. To be quite honest I couldn't believe that my brother, Alby would stay away from us, and I really did expect him to come back home the following night. However, the days and months went by, and there was still no sign of him. Whilst my mother went into a decline, my father seemed to me to become angrier, and appeared to have cut my brother completely out of his life. I missed my big brother so much I used to cry myself to sleep at night, completely unaware that my mother was not eating and was in fact quite ill!

It was a very cold and blustery night in the middle of November and I was playing in the front room (the parlour as it was known) with my friend Tommy Edgar. The wind was howling down the chimney, and it was an ideal night for playing ghosts and frightening each other. We were both taking turns at turning the light on and off and making ghostly sounds, when all of a sudden there was a piercing popping sound echoing from an antique cabinet my father had bought in an auction some weeks before, and then almost immediately the room fell into darkness. I flicked the light switch several times, but the light just refused to go back on. My friend, Tommy, called my attention to a bright light that had suddenly appeared above the cabinet. We stood speechless, mesmerised by its intensity, and riveted to the spot. The light gradually metamorphosed into the image of a lady draped in a long gown. As we watched in amazement, the image grew in size and became animated. At this point Tommy began to cry and made a dash across the room, pulling frantically at the door handle until the door finally swung open and he was free to make a hasty retreat.

I stood watching the ghostly apparition that now to me looked like Our Lady. She began moving her arms and smiling at me, and at this point just looked like a projected image on the wall. Gradually, though, the image became three-dimensional and looked so life-like, and the lady's angelic features became more apparent. I ran from the room to fetch my mother, father and aunt. 'Come quickly!' I called excitedly. 'Our Lady is next door.' I recall the look on my mother's face as she came with my aunt to investigate. My father, however, being the sceptic he was, remained in his armchair with his feet on the stool, completely disinterested in what was taking place in the adjacent room.

My mother and Aunt Sadie stood in front of the apparition wide-eyed and speechless. My mother immediately decided that if I touched it I would be cured of my illness. She moved a chair over to the cabinet and made me stand on it. 'Reach out and touch her,' she said quietly, holding the chair with one hand and steadying me with the other. I reached out, but before my hand made contact with it there was another popping sound and the apparition disappeared. Almost simultaneously the light came on in the room by itself. My mother and Aunt Sadie stood there staring at the wall in silence. 'What's happened?' I asked, somewhat confused. 'Where has the lady gone?'

My mother noticed a film of iridescent pink powder all across the surface of the old cabinet. Thinking that it had some connection with the apparition, she carefully collected it into an empty pill bottle. The following afternoon a neighbour brought two nuns from the local Catholic Church to see the place where the apparition had appeared. My mother retrieved the pill bottle to show them the pink powder, but to her amazement it had completely disappeared without trace. They prayed in front of the spot where the lady had appeared, and they told my mother we had been quite fortunate. 'This was a very special Mother coming to tell a mother that everything would be alright,' was one of the nun's explanations. 'You have been very blessed.'

Although my mother was obviously comforted by the apparition and what the nuns had said, it did seem to precede a sequent of unhappy events. A few weeks later I was admitted to Alder Hey Hospital with lobar pneumonia and my mother became very ill. In fact, the apparition seemed to be some sort of omen and for the months that followed our family went through an extremely unhappy period. Nonetheless, The Lady of Light was probably the most significant paranormal experience I have ever had in my whole life, and certainly one that I will never forget.

Although we didn't know it then, my brother, Alby, was to be away from us for nearly six years, and I was about fifteen when he came back into our lives. It goes without saying then that he is completely unaware of what exactly went on in my life during that period.

WHEN IS A DEAD MAN NOT A DEAD MAN?
Although by the age of six I had become quite accustomed to seeing things no body else could see, the first time I ever actually saw someone die in front of me was quite a bizarre experience. I was on my way home from a friend's house and was making my way through a narrow alley, which led directly into my road. There was a tall elderly man dressed in an overcoat and wearing a trilby walking in front of me, and a lady pushing a pram behind me. Suddenly, without any prior warning, the man in front of me slumped to the ground and just lay there still and silent. The lady behind me immediately rushed to his assistance and was soon joined by two other men. As I stood watching all the commotion, the man who had collapsed suddenly rose to his feet and walked slowly away. I did a double take, because his body was still lying on the cold ground, still and lifeless. He was obviously

dead and I had witnessed his spirit body moving away surrounded by a bright light. I watched in complete and utter amazement as the man's spirit body gradually disappeared into nothingness. I rushed home to tell my mother what had happened, so excited I was barely able to speak. Fortunately, though, my mother understood exactly what I had seen and just calmly reassured me and told me not to worry. 'He'll be alright now,' she told me. 'He's gone home.' That was probably the first time I had witnessed that sort of phenomenon and an experience that will always stay with me.

The long periods I spent either in hospital or in bed sick at home meant that I had the opportunity to focus my attention on the unseen things that were happening around me. I am quite certain that imagination forms a bridge between the consciousness and the reality of the Spirit World. Without imagination I am quite sure the psychic faculties could not function as efficiently, and spending so much time alone most certainly encouraged the cultivation of my image making faculty. Even when I wasn't 'seeing' so called 'dead' people I was watching images forming in the patterns on the curtains or wallpaper. In fact, I saw something in everything and always used my imagination as a means of escaping from this world. Little wonder then that music became my first love and played an integral part in my early life as a young adult.

CHAPTER THREE
MY FAMILY ORIGINS

My mother and her mother before her were mediumisti-
cally inclined, and my mother's mother, my Nanny
Walker, had many premonitions about things that were going
to happen. This ability was passed on to my mother, although
she always claimed that it frightened her a little. Nanny
Walker was of German origin, and her own parents could
speak very little English. Nanny Walker's aunt lived on a
farm in Aachen in Germany, and during the Second World
War she mysteriously disappeared after Hitler confiscated
her farm. My mother always believed that she was placed in
a concentration camp where she obviously died.

My mother's father, Jack Walker, had been killed in the
First World War. Apparently he was a veritable giant of a man
whose temper was quite explosive when he was drunk, which
was often. He had originally gone away to sea and was due to
sail on the Lusitania, but luckily for him he got drunk and
the ship sailed without him. He joined the army and was
killed anyway. It looked like big Jack Walker couldn't win,
and was destined to be killed whatever he did.

Although mum did not remember her real father – she was
only one when he was killed – her mother had told her all
about him and she had a couple of black-and-white photos of
him which she would speak to when she was feeling down.
She felt she knew him and this feeling brought her comfort.

Nanny Walker was left with four young children to bring
up, two girls and two boys, and no means of support.
Desperate measures were called for, and so she got a job as
barmaid in the Bronte Public House, quite close to where
they lived in Nesfield Street, Anfield. It was there she met

Billy Eden, a bricklayer and confirmed bachelor. Within a very short space of time he had moved in to their very small terraced house and they got married within two months.

My mother's stepfather was something of an unstable character. He just about tolerated his step children but when alcohol got the better of him, which it often did, he would lash out at them physically as well as verbally. Once Nanny Walker had children to Billy Eden his dislike of his stepchildren became more apparent. He made quite certain that his two daughters, Sadie and Mary, got preferential treatment over everybody else.

One day when my mother was 12 years old, her stepfather had been drinking and was in a particularly aggressive mood. For no apparent reason the sight of his stepdaughter washing the dishes incensed him and he grabbed hold of her by her forearms and began to shake her violently, yelling into her face at the same time. Fear and anger lent my mother strength and she struggled free of his grip and ran out of the kitchen and up the narrow staircase. Cursing her, her stepfather stumbled after her and mounted the first couple of stairs. She was nearly at the top by this time, and she stopped, heart pounding, and looked back at him. To her surprise he was standing immobile, staring up at the top of the stairs. As she looked, the blood drained from his face, leaving it ashen. She whipped her head around, following her stepfather's gaze and there she saw, with a jolt that ran through her body like electricity, the figure of a man standing at the top of the stairs. He wore a blue, collarless shirt, open at the neck, and black, baggy trousers, held up by a thick brown leather belt. He had strong square features, with very dark hair and a thick moustache, and seemed to be in his mid-thirties. He leaned forward slightly, ignoring my mother, and slowly raised a fist in the direction of her stepfather. The menacing expression on the apparitions face was unmistakable.

19

With a strangled cry, her stepfather fell back, tripped and landed heavily on the cold stone floor at the bottom of the stairs. My mother had flattened herself against the stairway wall in fright – she was trembling. She heard the crash as her stepfather fell below her and his groans and curses, but she kept her eyes fixed on the figure with the raised fist. It didn't linger, though, and in seconds had faded away into nothing.

My mother's stepfather was none the worse physically, apart from a bruise or two, and although the incident did not make him into a reformed character, it did make him think twice before lashing out at his stepchildren again. He never, ever, referred to the incident afterwards. Although the whole episode had lasted probably only a minute, my mother had recognised the figure on the stairs. It was her father, big Jack Walker, come to protect his child and to warn her stepfather to mend his ways.

My mother's older sister Louise was particularly mediumistic and had seen 'spirit people' since she was a child. She became interested in the embryonic Spiritualist movement in the 1930s and spent all her free time reading about spirit communication and mediums, and developing her own mediumistic abilities. In fact, Louise became known to all the family as the eccentric one, and she made no secret of the fact that she attended physical circles and direct voice séances, and had experienced ectoplasm and apports. Eventually Aunt Louise became cut off from the family, convinced that her path led in a different direction, and for many years no one saw her to speak to, although every so often news of her doings would filter back to them. In fact, Aunty Louise had lived all over the UK and had sat in circles with some of the well-known veterans of Spiritualism. She spoke often of the great Estelle Roberts and how at one time she had sat with her and witnessed the veteran medium's spirit guide, Red Cloud. Aunty Louise had been a policewoman most of her life, and had driven an ambulance through Blitz-torn Liverpool. She one told me that during the black out a spirit light would illumine her way, guiding her carefully through the rubble and bomb craters. In fact, Aunty Louise was instrumental in guiding me into Spiritualism and so played an important part in my life and early work as a medium. Sadly, she passed away a few years ago, but she was most definitely a significant 'signpost' along my way.

My dad's family were completely different. He had three brothers and one sister, and his mother, my grandmother Jane Roberts, married my grandfather, William Walmsly, 29 years her senior. She was Jewish and he was Welsh, and together they ran a pet shop at the back of St John's Market in the Liverpool City Centre, and this was where my father and his siblings were born. Two of my father's brothers, Charlie and Freddy, died in the 1930s when they were only in their early thirties. Because of this my father always feared that he would die of the same disease, bowel cancer, when in actual fact he died in 1970 of stomach cancer when he was 66. My father's other brother, George was in his early nineties when he died fairly recently. My grandmother suffered from senile dementia, and for a while lived with us in Grosvenor Road. Whatever went on between my father and his siblings caused a huge rift in the family, and when my grandmother passed away he took his share of the family business and never saw his sister ever again. Uncle George however came to make his peace with my dad just before he died. My father was dying of stomach cancer and his brother brought him a bottle of whisky – I could never understand that.

Recently my wife and I have started our family tree, and quite a few skeletons have popped out of the cupboard. I am sure there is more to come. They do say you can choose your friends but not your family. How true that is.

On a more pleasant note, I recently received an email from a lady living in Manchester called Antonia Mackenzie. She and her brother were doing their family tree and she had discovered that she was related to me. Antonia's father, Tony Skellon was the son of Freddie Roberts, one of my father's brothers who died sometime in the 1930s. I was even more intrigued when she told me that she was a registered hypnotherapist and that she ran a Complementary Therapy Centre in Sale, Manchester. Although a different area to the field I work in, the two are spiritually connected. She then went on to tell me that when she was younger she dated my cousin, Phil Roberts, only to discover that she was in fact related to him. I had never met my cousin Phil, and so I was fascinated by her story and very keen to meet up with them all. As this meeting only took place on Saturday just gone, I have had to interject this piece into the manuscript, hoping that you will see that there are innumerable coincidences in the story of my life. I now have family that I didn't know I had.

The most astounding revelation was when I discovered that my parents only married the month before my father died in 1970. I suppose I was more upset over the fact that I was not told, and was not privileged to be at their wedding.

CHAPTER FOUR
MY CHILDHOOD
IN LIVERPOOL

Although today I live in the very picturesque village of Lower Heswall, Wirral, quite close to the Dee Estuary, Liverpool will always be my spiritual home. Until recently my office was in Penny Lane (of Beatles fame), which meant that I travelled through the Mersey Tunnel to Liverpool at least four times a week. At least this kept me in touch with my Liverpool roots and gave me the opportunity to drive nostalgically through my old stamping grounds. Even though Lower Heswall is just across the River Mersey it's still not Liverpool. In fact, no matter where I have lived I have always been drawn back to Liverpool and frequently return to Grosvenor Road where I lived and grew up as a child. Sadly, like many other parts of Liverpool Wavertree is not the same. Although number 30 Grosvenor Road where I lived is still exactly the same, everything else has changed. The 'corner shops' have nearly all disappeared, the old neighbours I once knew have either died or moved on. All the back entries (jiggers) now have gates to prevent intruders, (a sign of the times unfortunately,) and a new estate of boxed-shaped houses has been built in Ash Grove and Wavertree Vale where prefabs once stood. These were the friendly little roads I used to explore when I was a child, and where Margaret Davies' Dairy was at the corner of Ash Grove. In the fifties the dairy had milking cows, and every week Margaret Davies and her husband could be seen herding them along the streets of Wavertree to graze for an hour or two in Wavertree Park, or the 'Mystery' as it was affectionately known. I often wonder how the neighbours put up with the cacophony of the cows mooing and the hens clucking.

In those days Mister Whippy had not yet been born, and a guy riding a bike with a small icebox in front, ringing a bell to let everyone know he was coming, delivered ice cream. There was no such thing as mobile phones or walkie-talkies then, and the beat bobby would either blow his whistle or bang his wooden baton on the pavement to catch his colleague's attention.

As a child in the fifties the streets of Liverpool were still badly scarred as a result of the Second World War. In fact, no street was untouched and bomb craters could be seen everywhere. I am old enough to remember the food being rationed, and can even recall my mother pushing me in my pram to a shop opposite Penny Lane to collect my powdered baby milk and small bottles of concentrated orange juice. We don't realise just how spoilt we are today, with restaurants and fast food take-aways. Where I grew up in Grosvenor Road, Wavertree, Abbott's Chip shop was only open on Thursdays and Saturdays. What they did the rest of the week I will never know.

In the fifties pupils would be called to school with the toll of a bell, and Lawrence Road School in the road adjacent to where I lived, had a huge clanging bell that could be heard for miles.

I can remember being in the corner shop with my mother when Mr Gamble, the shop's proprietor announced that King George V had died. I think I was seven at the time, and I had no idea that the King was even ill. All that I knew was that my mother seemed quite upset.

The Queen's Coronation was an amazing occasion, with bunting and street parties everywhere. Long trestle tables lined every street, with excited faces staring wide-eyed at the cakes and jellies. Every child received a Coronation mug and a commemorative penknife, and if you were lucky some kind lady would let you have two of each. As my place at the table was right outside my front door, I was able to take mine into the house and pretend that I hadn't received any at all.

Then came the threat of war with the Suez Canal Crisis, with everyone talking about the tyrant, President Nasser. The Second World War had only been over a few years, and already there was talk about a third one. I remember groups of jet planes constantly flying across the skies, and the air across Wavertree Park (the Mystery as it was affectionately known,) being cluttered with many Barrage Balloons. But then there was always the good old Penny Lolly Ice from Boyle's corner shop. I don't think Mrs Boyle ever forgave me for knocking on her door to buy one every Sunday evening. In the summer we used to watch the cockroaches crawling happily over the cream cakes in the glass case standing in the window.

In the fifties there seemed to be a shop on every corner. I remember mother going into the corner shop to buy butter, cheese and peas. Both the butter and cheese were in large slabs, which the shopkeeper would carefully slice with a wire cutter. Dried peas and butterbeans were sold from a large green container standing beside the counter. In those days the rules of hygiene were extremely slack and certainly left a lot to be desired. Nearly all food stood uncovered until the end of the day when everything was placed either under glass, or simply covered with a cloth of some sort.

I don't know whether we just look back through nostalgic rose-tinted glasses, but the summers always seemed to be much hotter then. Whenever they laid new road surfaces, the tar used to melt under the burning heat of the sun, and bubbles would form between the stone chippings across the road's surface. All the kids used to collect discarded Lolly Ice sticks, burst the tar bubbles with them and roll the melted tar onto the end of the sticks. Once this was done, the missiles would be thrown as high as we could to the top of the gable end wall, seeing who could make the most tar bombs stick to the brickwork. Old Mr Hodson was forever chasing us, either because of the mess we'd made of his wall, or because of the annoying noise of our ball kicked against the gable end wall.

Unlike today, policemen always seemed to be veritable giants and either Irish or Scottish. And Nuns were always attired in very long habits that framed their angelic faces and went right down to their feet. In those days nuns most certainly looked more religious and angelic than they do today, and they too always seemed to be Irish.

In our road the Protestants lived on one side, and the Catholics all seemed to live on the other. As a small boy I used to watch the priest as he called to every house in turn on a Sunday morning. A nun always accompanied him as he entered the open door of each house without even knocking. 'It's only me,' he would call. I could always tell when somebody had no money to give him because their front door would be closed. The priest would angrily knock on the closed door, and before moving on to the next house he would mark the person's name in his little book. No doubt they would have to have a good excuse and pay twice as much the following Sunday.

CHAPTER FIVE
MY SICKLY CHILDHOOD
AND MUSIC

Because I had suffered with Bronchiectasis since I was three, I suppose it is only right to say that I knew no different. This debilitating condition deprived me of a normal childhood, and whilst I did have lots of friends, I was never really allowed to play out during the winter months, in case I contracted pneumonia. Besides, I spent most of my life either in Alder Hey Children's Hospital, or in bed at home listening enviously to the other children playing and having fun in the street. Bronchiectasis is a symptom of cystic fibrosis, and although I did not have cystic fibrosis, I did have to do postural drainage several times a day (and still do). This meant my mother had to administer postural drainage, a procedure that involved my back being pummelled whilst I was lying in a horizontal position. This procedure had to be performed several times a day in order to keep my lungs clear of mucus and therefore free of infection. Not only did this make me extremely tired, but it was also quite inconvenient, particularly when my parents had visitors. Besides all that, I hated doing it, and the whole process made me feel abnormal and quite different.

Alder Hey Hospital was a very special place to me. I always had the same bed on Mary Two Ward every time I was admitted, and always with a clear view of the ward entrance, so I could see my mother coming through the door at visiting time each night. I was admitted into hospital three to four times a year, and had to spend at least six to eight weeks there on each occasion. This was the early 1950s when the treatment for such a condition was very limited, and when antibiotics were not as plentiful as they are today. Whilst I was in hospital I would have a Bronchogram, a procedure whereby a special powder was sprayed into my lungs so that they could be x rayed clearly and much more efficiently. I would have to be anaesthetised, and even that was quite traumatic for me. The only good thing about a Bronchogram was that once it had been done I would be discharged three days later.

Between the ages of seven and nine I suppose I became much more aware of my stays in Alder Hey. The porters would some times transport my bed to a remote part of the hospital, where I would be placed in an empty ward by myself. This was obviously a disused ward, with old screens and other medical equipment strewn untidily all over the floor. I would remain there all morning by myself without any food or drink, until eventually a group of student doctors would come to examine me. Why this could not have been done in my own ward I shall never know. I can only say that this inflicted quite a lot of permanent emotional damage to me, and is something I have never been able to forget. To make things worse some of the windows had black shutters over them, blocking out most of the bright sunlight and making the empty ward more eerie.

On each occasion when I was taken to the empty ward, an elderly nurse in strange clothes frequently visited me. She would just ask me if I was all right, and her soft voice would comfort and reassure me when I was distressed. She told me her name was nurse Rose and that she used to work on that particular ward. I saw the elderly nurse on four separate occasions, and the last time she came to me she explained that she was moving away and would not be able to see me again. When the porter came to take my bed back to Mary Two Ward, he reached over and retrieved a red rose from my pillow. 'Where did you get this?' he asked, smiling. 'From your girlfriend I'll bet?' Nurse Rose was of course a spirit, and was most probably from another time.

In the 1950s trams were still running in Liverpool, and I would often lie on my hospital bed at night listening to the rat-at-tat-tat of their metal wheels as they moved rhythmically along the lines, until they finally screeched to a halt once reaching their destination outside the hospital gates. I was somehow comforted by their familiar, hypnotic sound that never failed to lull me to sleep.

In those days there was no such thing as a light dimmer switch. Once the night nurse came on duty, she would climb a stepladder and cover the light with a black shade. How things have improved.

Whilst in hospital I had frequent nightly spirit visitors, and would often be told off by the nurse for calling her when I was frightened.

Everything happened to me in Alder Hey Hospital, from being visited by spirit clowns with funny painted faces, to seeing the spirit of a child that had just died in the bed opposite mine. Although I enjoyed my sojourns in Alder Hey Hospital, I was always so happy to be discharged so that I could return home.

It became quite obvious to my school nurse that I was a little different to other children, and so an appointment was made for me to see a child psychologist. The two hour long consultation consisted of me being shown a series of abstract coloured pictures and shapes, after which I was asked to tell the lady doctor everything I could see in them. On the conclusion of the boring consultation, without raising her eyes once to look at me, the psychologist scribbled a few notes on a piece of paper. Her carefully thought out diagnosis was given to my mother with a reassuring smile. 'William is extremely sensitive, and very insecure with a vivid imagination!' She said, almost dismissively. Although the nice lady doctor was correct in her diagnostic assumptions, her smug prognosis was wrong! 'He will grow out of it!' I did not!

Of course, my mother took it all with a pinch of salt. In fact, I found out later that she only went along with it because they had intimated that I would have to go away for assessment if she refused to take me to see the psychologist.

Some time after that I began to realise that not all children were the same. I became extremely religious and, although I was not a Catholic, I attended Catholic religious instruction at school, until Miss McGreavy realised I was a protestant and put an end to my sojourn into Catholicism.

It was some time around 1954, when I was eight that my love of the guitar really began. Georgie Hill, one of my brother's friends had bought himself a Hofner guitar from Rushworth's music store in the Liverpool city centre, and told my brother to bring me to see it. The guitar was so big I could just about see over the top of it. However, it was still love at first sight, and from that moment I knew I wanted to be famous and play guitar in a Rock and Roll group. Once I had got my very own guitar I played it every spare moment. Being ill all the time meant that I had more time to practise my guitar, and so I even took it with me to bed. I listened to every record I could of different guitarists, trying desperately to pick out every note, and mimic every technique. As far as I was concerned I'd already served my apprenticeship as a budding musician, busking outside of local pubs where I lived in Wavertree, with my first instrument, the four-stringed ukulele my mother had bought me earlier. Now, though, I had a real guitar and the world was my oyster!

Being psychic as a child did cause a lot of problems for me, and also meant that I was terrified of the dark. The feeble glow of the night-light only sufficed to create more shadows in the corner of my room, and even tightly closing my eyes failed to shut out the ghostly images that constantly flashed through my mind. At times my life was quite miserable, and only my mother understood what I went through.

In the mid-fifties the music scene began to change quite

dramatically. Crooners such as Frank Sinatra and Dean Martin were being pushed aside by new Rock and Roll giants such as Bill Haley, and then the great, hip-swivelling Elvis Presley. My brother, Alby, had been responsible for my interest in music with his huge collection of 78rpm records and LPs, which he was always playing on the radiogram my father had bought in one of the local auction sales. In those days nobody made a lucrative living from being a medium, and it never crossed my mother's mind that the unusual skill that her son was obviously born with would one day be used as a credible career. However, music was a different kettle of fish, so to speak. Both my mother and father could see that I had an aptitude for the guitar, and decided that music would be a good career to pursue, just in case I did survive into adult life. And so, at the age of 14 I joined my very first group, The Apaches. My father decided he could no longer ignore my mother's pleas for him to buy me an electric guitar, necessary if I was ever to be taken seriously. My father being quite miserly, he reluctantly gave her £10 to buy me my very first electric guitar, but when we reached Rushworth in Whitechapel, in the Liverpool city centre, I was disappointed to discover that the cheapest electric guitar was £13. 10. 6. This was a single cutaway solid body Antoria, with one gold pickup and golden metal machine heads. My eyes feasted on the magnificent guitar, my heart pounding inside my chest with excitement. I wanted it more than I'd ever wanted anything in my whole life. My mother could see by the look on my face that she could not disappoint me. Taking firmly hold of my hand she quickly led me from the shop. Together we made our way down the road towards The Bon Marche, where my aunty Sadie worked as supervisor in the restaurant. Although aunty Sadie had very little money, she managed to scrape together the £3.10.6 that we so badly needed to buy the guitar. 'I'll make sure you get it back!' my mother assured her. 'I'll get it from Albert!'

I now had my first electric guitar and was ready to tour the world and make lots of money.

My group's very first booking was at the Saturday Night Dance at Anthony of Padua's Church Hall, Mossley Hill, not far from Sefton Park. The big brother of one of the guy's in the band drove us to the venue in his van. To be honest, we did not need a van, as our equipment consisted of two small amplifiers and three guitars. We had no drummer, no bassist and no sound system! The hall was absolutely full to capacity, with a very loud band already playing. They were obviously very professional, all in their twenties, resplendent in gold lame suits, with greased-back hair and playing expensive Fender Stratocaster guitars. At fourteen I was the youngest in our band. I was so nervous that my heart was pounding heavily inside my chest, and beads of perspiration were trickling down my face. The group finished their set to a tumultuous applause, and within no more than five minutes we had set up and were ready to begin. 'Where's your drums?' Someone joked. We must have looked hilarious as we stood nervously before the crowds of Saturday night boppers. We started our first number, a Buddy Holly one I recall, but as soon as everyone started to dance, the sound of our music was lost completely under the noise of the shuffling feet across the wooden floor. Everybody stopped dancing and just booed us. 'Off! Off! Off!' They chanted, louder and louder until the mantra reached a piercing, aggressive crescendo. I quickly unplugged my guitar and collected my tiny amplifier into my arms, and then without looking back, I ran from the hall to the waiting van outside.

We travelled home in disappointed silence, our dream of becoming pop stars completely shattered. I personally felt as though the bottom had fallen out of my world. One by one we were dropped off at our respective homes. My parents were waiting patiently for me to arrive home, but I was too devastated to even face them. I ran upstairs to my bedroom, threw my guitar in the corner, and then buried my head in the pillow so mum and dad couldn't hear me crying. I secretly pledged that I would not play the guitar ever again! After my mum had consoled me, I remained in bed and fell into a deep sleep. I slept soundly that night completely oblivious to what was going on in the corner of my room. My mother had woken my father to listen to the sound of twanging guitar strings. Although it was the early hours of the morning they didn't mind me playing my guitar – or so they thought. My mother decided to investigate and went to peep in my room. To her amazement I was sound asleep, and yet unseen hands were plucking the strings on my guitar. The noise eventually woke me and I was amazed to see this eerie phenomenon and knew immediately who was responsible. I could see Tall Pine's silhouette in the shadowy corner of the room. My mother just smiled and quietly closed the door. I knew then that I must not allow anything to dishearten me. I had to carry on with the one thing I loved in life – playing the guitar. Nothing else mattered. I snuggled down beneath the covers, a contented grin across my lips, and fell once again into a deep sleep.

CHAPTER SIX
MUSIC REALLY MAKES
AN ENTRANCE

Little did I then know that the thing I loved most in the world would eventually nearly bring about my downfall. In 1962 at the age of sixteen, I was in a professional band, and already doing what every other teenager was only dreaming about – playing lead guitar in a fairly successful band. I was then in a band called THE CITY BEATS and my father had entered us in The Liverpool Echo's FRANKIE VAUGHAN TALENT COMPETITION, auditions to be held at Crane Hall (later called The Neptune Theatre) in the Liverpool, City Centre. We were competing against 2000 other musical acts, all wanting to be famous. The first prize was a recording contract and several thousand pounds worth of group equipment. The auditions took place every evening for the following two weeks, and each evening more contestants were eliminated from the competition. Each act was given a number, and we were given number 18. Every night we sat patiently waiting to see if we had been eliminated and each night our number was called, putting us forward to the following evening. Eventually we went through into the finals held on the South Pier at Blackpool. Also taking part in the show were the singers Ivor Emanuel and Doug Sheldon, the rock singer. Unfortunately we came third in the competition. Although we didn't know it at the time, a clapometer decided on the winner – which was the band Deny Seaton and the Sabres, a lively Rock and Roll Band with a huge following.

Extremely disappointed that we had gone all that way and still only come third in the competition, I took the offer to join the Kruzad s, a Rhythm and Blues Band, founded by singer Dixie Dean and bassist Eddie Hill. Their drummer was absolutely rubbish, and so I suggested that they bring in Danny Bell, the young drummer from my previous band, the City Beats. Danny was an incredible drummer, only twelve years old, and when he wasn't behind his kit of Premier Drums, he could always be found playing out in the street with his friends. Danny was like my baby brother, and once he was in the Kruzads we were like one big happy family. From then on my life as a musician changed dramatically. We were all eager to be successful, but equally knew that we needed a manager to handle our affairs. Mersey Sounds was probably one of the biggest agencies in Liverpool. Their offices were located in Lord Street, the Liverpool City Centre. Dixie contacted musical agent and entrepreneur, Sam Leach of MERSEY SOUNDS, who agreed to send one of his people to listen to us at one of our gigs. Gordon Brown came to hear us at Edge Hill Boy's Club, and he loved our sound and the look of us so much, that he immediately decided to take on our personal management. Gordon was slightly built but full of energy. He had been a professional boxer and had also won awards for Jiving. He was like a father to us all, and although he was quite fun loving and easy-going, he did tend to rule us with a disciplined rod of steel. We all loved Gordon, and I have no doubt that he loved us. In no time at all he had us touring extensively, playing as many as four gigs a day, and not finishing until 5 in the morning. I was completely exhausted and felt as though I needed a break from everything. We were playing at an all-nighter in Manchester when a black guy approached me during the break. 'Hi,' he said smiling, proffering a hand. 'My name's Johnny Firefly. You look like you probably feel. Try some of these.' He dropped about eight purple tablets onto the palm of my hand and passed me a bottle of Coke. 'Take three for now,' he said grinning. 'Take some more later.

They'll give you a lift, man.' Johnny Firefly was right. It was just after 3.30 in the morning and I felt as though I could go on playing forever. I felt so full of energy and was ready for anything. Johnny and I became good friends, and every time we played at the club he would always be there to make sure I had what I needed to get me through the night. In fact, it was Johnny who gave me my very first introduction to cocaine, and from then on it was all down hill, although it didn't seem like that at the time. It got so bad that I really could not wait until we played in Manchester for some form of narcotic substance to keep me going, and so I just knew I had to find another source. Although up until the age of 19 I used cocaine and amphetamine substances recreationally, I always knew that deep down there was a deeper craving that would one day go completely out of control. Looking back I now know that it was my father who kept me under control. He wasn't the easiest man to talk to and had an extremely volatile personality. Although even as a child he never ever laid a hand on me, he always kept me in check, and whilst I lived under the same roof as him I knew I had to make sure I was always in control.

By the end of 1964 our band seemed to be playing 34 hours a day, at least, that's how it felt to me. On one particular and very rare occasion I arrived home at 10.30pm and was just about to have an early night when the phone rang. 'Billy,' said the familiar voice of our manager, Gordon Brown, 'Be ready in 20 minutes we are going to a party – a very special party.'

'But...' I stuttered tiredly, trying to tell him I wanted an early night.

'Just be ready!' Before I could say another word the line went dead.

Gordon picked me up as arranged and drove me to the Tuebrook Bowling Alley. He looked quite excited and said we were going to have some publicity photos taken. The bowling alley had closed for the night but it had been booked for a private party. Gordon was extremely secretive and kept grinning mischievously. As soon as we walked into the bowling alley I stopped in amazement - it was The Rolling Stones. I couldn't believe it. This was 1964 and the Stones were already quite big. 'Come on, Billy, I'll introduce you to the boys.' Gordon's brother-in-law, Sam Leach, had booked the Stones to do a gig at the famous Locarno Ballroom and had hired the bowling alley for the night to help them unwind. Also there was Marianne Faithful, and the black singing duo, Inez and Charlie Fox. I had some publicity photos taken with the Stones, and Mick Jagger wanted to buy my waistcoat. I had to decline and told him that my mother had made it. When I told her this later she went mad. 'You should have given it to him,' she said proudly. 'It would have been nice to see Mick Jagger wearing the waistcoat I made.'

This was the original Rolling Stones, with Brian Jones before he tragically died in a swimming pool at his home. We were with them until around four in the morning, so I still did not manage to have an early night. Still, it was really nice to spend the night with the Stones, my favourite band at that time. Dixie Dean, one of the singers in the K ruzads, was furious when he heard where we'd been. Dixie was like a big brother to me, and he was a huge fan of the Stones. Although he was annoyed with me, our manager, Gordon Brown, explained that it wasn't my fault, and that there would not have been enough time to pick him up. Dixie was ok then, and just wanted to know all about the Rolling Stones and what they were like.

The Kruzads already had a huge following all over the northwest, and we were playing as many as five venues a day some weeks. Although it was quite exhausting we really did have a great time. Although Gordon was our manager we occasionally got work from other agents. Abensterne Promotions in Hanover Street, in the Liverpool City Centre, phoned me to ask if we could do a spot on the Club Ship Landfall, from 9pm until 10pm. This was a small boat that had survived the Dunkirk Landings, and had been turned into a nightclub, and was moored somewhere in the Liverpool Docks 'If you can do it you'll have to play commercial stuff!' insisted Ted Lamb. 'The manager won't tolerate any of that loud Rhythm and Blues music!' Another agent, Ron Ellis, from Southport had already phoned to book us into the Peppermint Lounge in London Road, at 7.30pm for one hour, and then on to do a spot at the Klik-Klik Club in Southport at 10.30pm. This meant the Club Ship Landfall gig filled the nine till ten spot perfectly. 'Don't worry, Ted!' I said. 'We can play any kind of music!' He huffed disbelievingly before hanging up. The fee for the Club Ship Landfall was £15 a spot, a good fee in comparison to other venues. Needless to say, we only played two numbers when we were stopped. 'The manager wants to see you in his office.' The girl said. 'He doesn't look too happy!'

He was sitting at his desk, patiently waiting for me. 'Here,' he said, pushing an envelope across the polished surface of the desk. 'There's £15, you can go now!' Although disappointed that he didn't like our music, at least we got paid for doing practically nothing. This now gave us plenty of time to get to our next gig.

Shortly after this our manager, Gordon, introduced us to Mal Jefferson, a bass player and singer from a band called The Master Sounds, who had just returned from Hamburg. Mal was an incredible blues singer, and Gordon persuaded us to let him join the band. From then on our music changed, and so too did our popularity. First of all our bass player, Eddie Hill left, and then the founder member, Dixie Dean decided to call it a day. The Kruzads then became a self-indulgent band, totally controlled by Mal Jefferson.

EUROPE HERE WE COME

The K ruzads disbanded and I reformed the band with a different line-up. We had already been touring all over Europe, and so under new management the new band was ready to go. The music scene in Liverpool was quite saturated with different kinds of groups, everything was changing and the continent was crying out for the sound of Liverpool bands. We took off to Calais and arrived in the early hours of the morning. We checked in to a dirty looking hotel above a café on the waterfront. There were bugs in my bed so I slept all night in a chair and was woken by the sounds of mopeds and the general cacophony of French workers on their way to begin their daily chores on the docks. It was horrible and I wanted to go home. We had no more than fifty pounds between the four of us, and after the horrendous night spent in that uncomfortable and extremely filthy hotel we were all ready to head home on the first ferry. We decided to use the last of our money and make our way to Boulogne Sur Mer. We had no idea where we were going to stay, but one of the lads knew a hotel and was sure we would get some work there. THE HOTEL MAURICE was a three star hotel with its own nightclub called The Chat Noir. The Manager, a very tall and extremely over weight lady, took an immediate liking to us and gave us a residency in the club. She agreed to give us one room between the four of us and one meal a day and pay us five francs a night. As far as we were concerned this was a good offer. Anyway, it was preferable to admitting defeat and returning to the UK for everyone to laugh at us. We had an excellent time playing in the club and our sojourn there lasted the whole of the summer. Early in September the kind manageress informed us that The Chat Noir would be closing and that we would have to vacate our room within three days. However, she did tell us that she had a friend who was an agent and that he would be travelling from Belgium to listen to us. Jean Vanlou was one of the biggest musical impresarios on the Continent and managed some of the most successful names in French Music. We were all so excited and celebrated by spending what money we had left on a couple of bottles of French wine.

The following Monday afternoon Jean Vanlou arrived at the hotel with his entourage. He was an extremely over weight cigar-smoking Flemish man with an infectious smile. Although he himself spoke very little English, after we had exhausted our 30 song repertoire, Sammy, Jean Vanlou's assistant told us that Jean Vanlou liked us very much and that he wanted us to move to Mouscron in Belgium the following afternoon.

Mouscron was a small town with cobbled streets and very friendly people. Jean Vanlou's secretary checked us into a small hotel in the town centre, and in the evening we were taken to Jean Vanlou's club, The Twenty Club, apparently the 'Hottest Spot' in town. As soon as we began playing to a capacity audience everyone went crazy. Jean Vanlou was amazed at the way we had gone down and at the end of the evening we celebrated with a few bottles of Champagne.

We were resident at the Twenty Club for six months with no signs of playing anywhere else. The band began to get a little restless, and although there was a never-ending queue of 'groupies' there was little else to do in Mouscron, once the lights went out and shutters came down. Little wonder then that we all went off the rails. Jean Vanlou then told us that we must return home to the UK for three months until he sorted our visas and contracts. I must admit we were all extremely suspicious and thought that this was his way of getting rid of us. We didn't expect to be coming back and went a bit wild in the hotel that night. My friend Steve Barton and I leaned incoherently against a huge ornate mirror in the foyer of the hotel and then watched in amazement as a crack suddenly appeared across its surface and it smashed to the floor in three pieces. The hotel receptionist was horrified and the manager demanded payment immediately. Not having any spare cash, and thinking that we would not be returning to Mouscron, Steve and I signed an agreement to pay for the damaged mirror within four weeks. As far as we were concerned that was the end of the matter and we returned home to the UK.

We had been home two weeks when Jean Vanlou telephoned to say that he wanted us to return to Belgium at the end of the month to begin a tour of venues all over Europe. Along with a new road manager and an additional member to the band, keyboard player Stevie Doyle, we set off once again to Belgium. However, this time was completely different – we had contracts and an extensive tour with some of the biggest names in the world of music.

This time we stayed in a little town called Comines again in Belgium. We stayed in a hotel that had been empty since the Second World War and was being refurbished. There was a nightclub on the ground floor, and during the week we were to rehearse there. Jean Vanlou gave strict instructions that we were NOT to go behind the bar or even think of touching any alcohol. The temptation was too great and within five days we had nearly consumed most of the spirits and drunk at least two barrels of lager. Jean Vanlou had been away on business and on his return he went ballistic! He gave us the option of either returning to the UK or paying for what we had drunk. We had too much to lose and so we decided to stay and pay for the alcohol we had consumed.

To make the whole situation even worse, Steve Barton and I had just left the club and were making our way down the road towards a local bar. A white Volkswagen Beetle car pulled up and two men jumped out holding warrant cards in front of us. 'Monsieur Billy Roberts – Monsieur Steve Barton?' One of the men asked sternly. We nodded and were immediately handcuffed and bundled into the back of their car. We were arrested for the broken mirror in the hotel and thrown into a cell for the rest of the night. Because no one in the police station could speak any English – or so they had said – we had to wait until they found someone who could. Eventually, Jean Vanlou was called to bail us out. Against his better judgement he paid for the mirror plus some costs and took us back to his office to scold us. Jean Vanlou was a huge man in every sense of the word. Although he was very kind and gentle, he did have a temper and demanded respect. Needless to say we did appreciate Jean Vanlou's fatherly protection and did pay every Franc back to him, even though it took quite a long time. I've got to admit, this Flemish musical entrepreneur obviously had a special fondness for the Kruzads and showed it in every way possible. However, his agency was expanding and every French band wanted to be managed by Unidans, Jean Vanlou's company. We did get the feeling that he had taken too much on, and Sammy, Jean Vanlou's closest friend, intimated that Jean was considering joining forces with an agent from Spectre Promotions. This meant the whole situation would change and the close relationship we had with Jean Vanlou would not be the same. We knew it was only a matter of time before the bubble would burst and we'd be forced to return home to the UK. I was right, and within weeks we had to return to the UK once again, 'Until your permits have been renewed!' said Jean Vanlou. 'It will be for no longer than two weeks!'

CHAPTER SEVEN
SEX DRUGS AND ROCK
AND ROLL

Jean Vanlou was telling the truth, and in just over two weeks we were back on the Continent. As far as I was concerned now we were really on the road to fame and making a lot of money. All my childhood dreams were at long last coming true. Not only had he arranged an extensive tour, covering France, Belgium, Germany and Sweden, but he had also secured a recording contract for us with Vogue International. We did not care so much about the money we could potentially earn, as we did about the kudos of playing with such big names. Our first gig was at an event in Brussels, called Wolu City. There we were to play in a huge marquee before ten thousand people, who had travelled to the massive prestigious event from all over the world. The year was now 1966 and the very festive event was 'The World's Fair', to be covered by media from many European countries. We were young, full of energy, naïve and very nervous. The World's Fair was on for a whole week, and many bands were appearing at the event. Although veritably unknown outside of the north west of England, on the Continent the Kruzads had a huge following and were now ready to set the marquee at Wolu City – The World's Fair – on fire. We were to support such musical giants as the British band, The Yardbirds (with Jeff Beck,) The Moody Blues, The Who, veteran black American blues singer, Memphis Slim, and a French 'Jug Band' by the name of Ferry Grenyard. Jean Vanlou had told us that we were to go on stage before The Yardbirds. We did three numbers, and could hardly hear ourselves playing because of the sound of chanting and screaming. At this point

I wasn't sure whether they loved or hated us, until we had concluded our set and the audience began chanting their rhythmical mantra of 'KRUZADS! KRUZADS! KRUZADS!' We couldn't believe it! We wanted to go back on stage, but Jean Vanlou said in no uncertain terms, 'FINNY! YOU ARE FINISHED!' We breathed a huge sigh of relief and looked forward to seeing our favourite band The Yardbirds play.

The Yardbirds took quite a long time setting up their equipment on stage. And then, to my surprise, their lead guitarist, Jeff Beck, asked if he could borrow my fuzz box – a little gadget used primarily to distort the sound of the guitar and make it funkier. I agreed, of course, but in the heat of my enthusiasm I forgot to mention to him that the battery in the device needed renewing. This meant that the overall sound of the guitar would lose its volume and sharpness. Halfway through the Yardbirds first song I noticed Jeff Beck glaring angrily at his amplifier. There was obviously something wrong with the sound. I watched from the side of the stage as the frustrated guitarist gesticulated to me, in an asserted effort to make me come to his rescue. However, before I realised exactly what was happening, the irate Jeff Beck had kicked his amplifier, and the two Marshall cabinets fell back from the stage causing an almighty 'crash'. Amidst all the commotion the band somehow managed to keep on playing, but on the conclusion of their set, the singer, Keith Relf, began shouting some obscenities at Jeff Beck. However, the ten thousand-strong audience was obviously oblivious to what was taking place in front of them, and The Yardbirds vacated the stage to a tumultuous applause. Backstage we discovered that Jeff Beck's Marshall cabinets had fallen on to our keyboard and caused a lot of damage. Completely disinterested by the damage he had caused, the unruffled Jeff Beck told our keyboard player to see his manager. However, he was nowhere to be found!

They do say that if you can remember the sixties you were

not there. I can't say that I remember it all, but I do occasionally find myself recalling the sixties with nostalgia. I suppose it's only fair to say that I spent most of the sixties somewhat out of my mind on some sort of narcotic substance. The only thing I can't remember is where exactly we obtained what we did to get stoned. After our gig with the Yardbirds we did get smashed. You can imagine how we felt when Jean Vanlou told us that The Moody Blues had not yet arrived, and so he wanted us to play another set. That part of the show was a complete and utter blur, and how we got through it I shall never know.

Although The Moody Blues were not my kind of band, they were exceptionally professional, and their huge sound filled every corner of the ten-thousand capacity marquee.

Wolu City was one of the biggest musical events in Europe and lasted for a whole week. People visited it from all over the world, and the seven-day festival was televised and broadcast all over Europe. We were to play the following day, just before The Who. To save money, all the lads in the band decided to sleep under one of the trailers parked along side the huge marquee, whilst our road manager, Gary Clampit and I checked into a hotel for the night.

As the Who were known for their rowdy and very boisterous reputation, we warned Paul not to touch anything belonging to them. 'They won't take it lightly!' I said. 'They'll give you a smacking!' Paul dismissed my words with a cheeky grin, telling me he'd already done the dastardly deed and taken his souvenirs. However, it wasn't until we had left the musical festival that that he produced his trophies – three pairs of leather boots belonging to the Moody Blues. That was Paul!

The Who were very loud and opened their set with one of their hits, Substitute, and concluded the show with My Generation. We watched in amazement as Pete Townsend smashed his guitar onto the wooden platform, and Ke ith

Moon, the drummer, demolished his drums, by kicking them all over the stage. Whilst the security men watched nervously, shaking their heads and not knowing whether or not to intervene, Paul stood at the side of the stage, waiting to seize the opportunity to rescue something from K eith Moon's devastation. All too soon this fantastic event was over, and we now had to make our way to Paris to support the incredible Chuck Berry.

John Thompson, one of our singers and I, left Brussels with our own souvenirs. Their names were Vivian Ville, and Martine D'meve, two beautiful Belgium girls who had followed us all over the Continent. Vivian Ville's father ran a huge company in Brussels, and her mother was a fashion journalist for a well-known fashion magazine. Both she and her friend, Martine, wanted John and I to live with them in Brussels, where they each had their own spectacular town house. They travelled with us to Paris, but when John and I lost interest in them they returned to Brussels. I kept in touch with Vivian for some years until she married a Dutch lawyer.

I am frequently asked what happened to my psychic skills all the years I was touring Europe with my band? They were still very much an integral part of my life, but my psychic energies were somehow channelled into the creative areas of my life. Although I did use them, often for my own ends, so to speak, I would occasionally have incredible, and yet, often terrifying psychic flashes, either forewarning me of something, or just simply reassuring me.

CHAPTER EIGHT
AND THE BEAT GOES ON

I loved travelling all over the continent, staying in hotels and playing in different clubs. It's funny, but back home in the UK we were just one of the thousands of veritably unknown bands struggling along to make a name for ourselves, but on the continent we were celebrities and had a huge following. All this was achieved in a very short time. Little wonder then that we went crazy.

CHUCK BERRY IN PARIS

From Brussels we moved to Paris to play at the famous La Locomotive Club, next to the Moulin Rouge. We had been booked to support the legendry Rock and Roll artiste Chuck Berry. We were all so excited to actually play on the same stage as the man responsible for hundreds of Rock and Roll compositions, many of which had been recorded by The Rolling Stones. On the evening of the show Chuck Berry's manager asked to see a list of our repertoire for the evening. After carefully checking it he informed us that we would not be allowed to perform the songs that Chuck Berry had composed. Then he asked, 'Chuck would like to use one of your amplifiers, if that's ok?' Although we felt privileged for this great performer to use our amp, personally I did think he had a cheek! Then, to add insult to injury, during the rehearsal Chuck Berry pulled his guitar lead from my amplifier and complained that it did not have the right sound for his style of playing. He ended up using our bass guitarist's amplifier saying it was 'cool!' Even though we never got so much as a 'thank you,' from Chuck Berry, Jimmy Iko, our bass guitarist was quite proud of the fact that his amp had been used and not mine.

One very hot sunny afternoon in 1967, whilst strolling through the back streets of Paris, we went into a Turkish restaurant for something to eat. The English speaking Turkish waiter invited us to join him with a few lines of cocaine and a couple of bottles of wine. I don't think he even charged us for the meal, and was also kind enough to hand me a little package as we left his restaurant.

JIMI HENDRIX

A few days later the lads had gone for a boat trip on the River Seine and I went with Jean Vanlou for drink and something to eat and to discuss the rest of the tour. By then The Kruzads had become well known and Jean Vanlou had already secured a record deal with Vogue International. After the meal we returned to the Locomotive Club to collect Jean's briefcase when he suddenly stopped to embrace two guys leaving the club. 'Jean, man,' said one of the guys in a soft American drawl, 'Nice to see you again.' I did a double take and for a moment was speechless. Jean Vanlou let go of the guy's hand and turned to me.

'Billy,' he began in his usually broken English, 'This is...'

'Jimi Hendrix.' I quickly interrupted. I couldn't believe it. Jimi was my hero and to my mind the world's greatest guitarist. His record, 'Hey Joe,' had soared to the top of the charts and had made him a household name. This was a blues number that had been written by my namesake – Billy Roberts – unfortunately, no connection.

'This is Billy Roberts,' Jean Vanlou introduced me. 'He plays lead guitar with my English band The Kruzads.'

'Hi Billy,' said Jimi, quickly remarking upon my name. 'Yeah, Billy Roberts. Good name, man.' Jean Vanlou invited Jimi and his friend to join us for something to eat, and all through the meal I just couldn't believe that I was actually sitting across the table from the great Jimi Hendrix. Jimi Hendrix was a gentleman and extremely charismatic, but I was overwhelmed with a strange feeling that he would not live very long. In fact, Jimi died of a drug overdose in 1970, and was a great loss to the world of music. Even to this day I can't believe that I actually had a meal with my hero, the guitar legend, the late Jimi Hendrix.

That afternoon with Jimi Hendrix was the highlight of my life. The rest of the guys were really angry that they had not joined us, and they knew they had missed the opportunity of a lifetime. Jean Vanlou had in fact brought Jimi Hendrix to the continent to play at the Twenty Club in Mouscron, and then to Paris where he played at two major venues, La Locomotive being one, and The Olympia being the other.

Good news came via Jean Vanlou's secretary, Sammy. Jean had secured a record deal for us, and we had two weeks to write two original songs. As I was the only one who wrote music, the onus was on me to create something. I wrote The Reason, a two part harmony number, and a rock number, entitled, The Devil Never Wins. I wrote them while we were in Paris, and although we just threw the songs together, Jean Vanlou was pleased with them. They wanted to record the band live at the Twenty Club, to capture the real sound of the Kruzads, and so it was decided that we would have to wait until our return to Belgium.

By now cracks were appearing in the band's friendship. Because John Thompson was by far the better singer, and possessed quite an extensive vocal range, Steve Barton held some resentment for him. They were always arguing, and because I was friendly with them both, and therefore refused to take sides, Steve began to fall out with me. The band split down the middle; Jimmy Iko, the bass player, Steve Barton and Paul Hitchmough formed one part of the split, and John and I the other. I became very depressed and no longer enjoyed playing in the band. Like it or not, we had contracts to fulfil, and so we had to get on with it!

CHAPTER NINE
THE GHOSTS OF DUNKIRK

Paris was an experience and one we would never forget. We had returned to where we were staying in Comines, and had recorded our record at The Twenty Club. Although it was very raw, we were all very pleased with it. It was Easter Friday and we had two days off. Our 'roadie' suggested that we should take a trip to Dunkirk to see where it all took place in the Second World War. I had always had a fascination with the historical side of the war and had even collected Second World War artefacts since I was very young, so I was quite excited with the prospect of visiting such a significant historical landmark. It took us some time to find it but we eventually reached Dunkirk. As soon as I set foot on the sands of Dunkirk Beach I was overwhelmed with a strange feeling of sadness and deep foreboding. It was an eerie place, and as I scanned the sandy terrain the feelings of sadness and foreboding became more intense. For a few moments I was lost in my own thoughts and my consciousness was somehow transported back to that famous battle in the latter days of the war. I found myself leaving the lads and making my way along the beach alone. I stooped and dug my hand deep into the sand and retrieved some spent bullet cases. I felt a cold chill pass over me and a darkness suddenly descended on the beach. As I stood there I could hear the sound of planes passing overhead and the rat-at-tat-tat of machine gun fire all along the beach. I peered over to where the German pillboxes were strategically situated all along the edge of the sand, and could see the dark silhouettes of German soldiers comfortably positioned, randomly picking off their helpless targets. I was transfixed and felt that I couldn't move from that spot even if I wanted to. The air was thick with both smoke and fear and I could hear the cries of the British soldiers as they fled for their lives towards the water's edge. My thoughts were sharply interrupted by a concerned voice, and the ghostly images of the war quickly dispelled. 'Are you alright?' an elderly man walking his dog asked. 'You've seen them haven't you?' He went on, speaking good English.

'Yes,' I answered. 'Why, have you?'

'Oh, yes,' he confirmed, nodding with a smile. 'I live on the waterfront in one of those large houses overlooking the beach, and have done so since I was a child. I remember it well.' He paused thoughtfully and bent down to stroke his patient dog. 'The ghosts of that awful battle will remain here forever. Terror like that does not go away. Many visitors to Dunkirk have seen them.' He bade me farewell and continued to walk with his dog further down the beach. I stood there for a few moments wondering if the lads had seen anything. They were still fooling around some way down the beach, completely oblivious to what I had been experiencing for the past 20 minutes or so. I clutched the empty bullet cases in my hand, and then placing them securely in my pocket, went to join the other guys further down the beach. That was an experience I will never forget. I had witnessed a sort of paranormal photographic replay of the events of Dunkirk, rather like watching a video or DVD.

Strictly speaking I did not 'see' the spirits of those who had fought on the beach during that awful battle. My mind had accessed a sort of memory bank, and I was able to experience the whole thing as though I was actually there in the midst of it all. Besides, many of those who took part in the evacuation of Dunkirk Beach would most probably have still been alive. Any intensely emotional event impregnates the atmosphere with a lasting impression. This is replayed over and over for onlookers to see, rather like watching an old monochrome movie time and time again. Fortunately for me it was a movie

I had not seen before, but one I would not like to see again.

That experience jolted my mind and made me remember the psychic abilities I had had since I was a child. Although my experience on Dunkirk Beach was objective – and anybody present could have seen what I had seen – the fact that the other guys in the band were oblivious to the whole eerie scenario, proved to me that I was meant to see what I had seen, if only to remind me of something that I had somehow pushed to the back of my mind – I had psychic skills and would one day have to use them.

My visit to Dunkirk made me realise that whilst I was working on the continent I was living in a paranormal mine field and must prepare myself for all psychic eventualities. My sensitivity meant that I would be more receptive to the vibratory atmosphere than the other guys in the band and must take measures to ground and protect myself. All this will probably seem far fetched and fanciful to a sceptic, but I was living in an atmosphere that had been created out of sadness, anxiety and trauma; emanations from the Second World War and the German occupation, and I did have to safeguard my sensitivity and tread with great caution. This was the reality I was living in, and although seeing so-called 'dead' people had always been commonplace to me, here I was forced to walk beside them in their own world, with no way whatsoever of 'turning' the whole thing off.

Where we were living in Comines there was an old church standing proudly in a very picturesque village square. Each time I walked across the cobbled square en-route to the café, something always pulled me to the wall at the far end of the church. One warm evening I had left the lads at the café and was making my way across the square back home to the place we were staying. As I reached the church I suddenly felt a little disorientated and found myself wandering over towards the gable end. I saw a frail looking old woman crying as she placed some flowers against the wall. As I couldn't speak

French very well I walked over towards her and just placed a comforting hand on her shoulder. She nodded to let me know she was alright, but her eyes were sad and faded with age, and I could see that her pale and lined face had not known happiness for many years. The old woman took a step back and glanced sadly at the wall. I followed her eyes to a particular spot and saw that there was a plaque marking a memorable event that had obviously taken place there. I wasn't sure whether I was feeling overwhelmingly sad because of the old woman, or whether there was another more subtle paranormal reason. I watched as the old woman crossed herself and muttered an almost soundless prayer, and then pointed to the plaque positioned more or less in the centre of the wall. I moved my eyes from the plaque back to the old woman but she had gone – disappeared without trace. I felt a shiver down my spine as I moved my eyes from one end of the church wall to the other, but the old woman was still nowhere to be seen.

The following afternoon I was talking to the woman in the local grocer's shop and telling her about my strange experience at the church wall. 'That is Marian,' she said immediately. 'She placed flowers at the wall till the day she died twenty years ago.'

'Till the day she died?' I gasped. 'She's dead? But I actually touched her.'

'Yes,' she smiled. 'You are not the first, and I doubt very much that you will be the last.' She continued to wrap the cheese I had bought. 'Her son and husband were in the Résistance and were executed at that wall by the Gestapo. She died of a broken heart. The plaque on the wall commemorates that horrible event and also explains that Marian Desprate died of a broken heart.' I was speechless. That was why the old woman was pointing to the plaque; she was trying to explain who she was. I felt privileged to have seen her and to have experienced that moment of deep sadness – a sadness that had broken the old woman's heart and brought her life to an end. That was another ghostly encounter during my sojourn on the continent, and I wondered if there was more to come.

If I said that my mediumistic skills have never caused me any problems, I would be lying. There were occasions when I have been deeply disturbed by my experiences, and frequently felt depressed. Although today I more or less have my psychic abilities under control, I know that it is something I could never turn my back on. Although the church decries mediums and psychics, I have always thought that this is the result of ignorance. I have always known that the Bible itself is based on the teachings propagated by prophets and wise men, and although the holy book as we know it today has been re-written to conform to the ever-changing face of Christianity, Christian fundamentalists are usually very selective in their choice of what sections of the Bible to quote. Mediums are born and most certainly not made. Although today I have had to refine my mediumistic skills, primarily to enable me to control and understand them, when I was a young boy my unusual skills controlled me. I have said before, I have sustained an awful lot of emotional and psychological damage because of my psychic skills, and although I have frequently tried to turn my back on them, I now know it would be easier to have all my limbs removed.

CHAPTER TEN
MY CAREER BEGINS
TO CHANGE

We were still resident at the Twenty Club in Mouscron, and still packed the place out every Sunday. It was then that I met Marie Paul Vancanagen. She was 17 and I had just turned 20. Her sister Monique was crazy about Steve Barton our second singer, but he was already spoken for and was engaged to Patsy, a girl back in England. Steve was in an emotional dilemma and just didn't know what to do. Steve and I had been friends since he was 14 and we had always been like brothers. I could see that he liked Monique and it would have been more convenient for me if Steve were with Monique. At least then we could have travelled to see them together. Eventually I managed to persuade Steve to get it together with Monique, and he decided to finish with Patsy on an extremely long telephone conversation the following day. In 1968 both sisters were pregnant. Marie Paul's English was not too good, but she was extremely volatile and I quickly got the gist of her displeasure. That was it as far as the relationship was concerned, and before we had begun our final tour it reached its natural conclusion and we went our separate ways.

The friction in the band was reaching incredible heights and everyone was arguing. Steve's growing dislike of John was affecting their singing. They were forever disagreeing over who was going to sing what. Although I tried desperately to stay neutral, I seemed to be forever in the middle. The arguments became more and more aggressive, and it was clear that we could not go on this way. It was around this time that Jean Vanlou announced that he had handed our management over to Ricki Stein from Spectre Promotions. He was a brash and very arrogant Londoner and was immediately disliked by the band. At this point we were staying in Comines in the refurbished hotel, and during the day we rehearsed in the club downstairs. Ricki Stein appointed a guy called Pier as our minder, and basically to ensure that we did not lie in bed all day. He was crazy, and his way of getting us out of bed was to fire a high powered air rifle at the bedclothes. This was extremely dangerous, but at least it got us out of bed!

Pier was quite menacing and had a sadistic temperament. We disliked him immensely, and pleaded with Jean Vanlou to get rid of him. 'It's no longer my responsibility!' he mumbled in broken English, puffing on his big cigar. 'Take your complaints to Ricki!'

Then, one morning it seemed that our luck had changed. Paul popped his head into my bedroom. 'Do you know what time it is?' He grinned. '10.30 and there's no sign of Pier.' No sooner had he said this than the police came to search Pier's room. His girlfriend was with them and she was crying. After they had left she told us that her boyfriend had attempted to rob a bank but had been caught in the act. She couldn't understand why we were all so pleased.

Our time was divided between Brussels and Paris, and we were becoming well known all over Europe with a huge following. We played with the Kinks and the Small Faces, and really felt as though we were at long last getting somewhere.

We had completed a mini tour with our last gig at Liege Football Club, and had finally sadly decided to disband and go our separate ways. After a lengthy discussion it was agreed that instead of returning to our base in Comines, that we would make our way back to the UK. We had completed a tour of seven venues and been paid cash at each one. This meant that we had Ricki Stein's commission and were expected to deliver this to his office on the following Monday.

This did not happen – we divided the money and returned home to England. First thing Monday morning Ricki Stein phoned me at my mother's house and went ballistic down the phone. He threatened that we would never work on the Continent ever again, and that he would do all in his power to make sure that we would pay for what we had done to him. I personally had no intention of returning to France or Belgium so it really did not matter.

In 1969 Marie Paul gave birth to a baby boy but vowed that I would never see him. At that point in my life I was too preoccupied with other things, and although I was pleased that I had a French son I had no intention of ever trying to see him. However, this all changed some years later.

When we lived on the continent there was always a never-ending line of girls waiting to be with us. We had women all over France, Belgium and Germany. They would often travel great distances just to be with us and stay in our hotel for a while. I know it sounds quite awful now, but I often got their names mixed up and sometimes even forgot their names completely. Although there were parts of the sixties I can't remember, I can recall most of it, and I can honestly say I would not have changed one thing.

After being out of the UK for so long, I did find it difficult to settle. Although I needed desperately to reform a new band, until I did I found myself 'between bands', as they say in the music business. My father made it clear to me that he did not want me lying in bed all day, and even suggested that I should get a 'real' job to get some money to pay for my keep. My father was a friend of the caretaker of Lawrence Road School just at the back of our house. Jimmy Rigby told my father he could get me the job as junior porter, and that the work would not be too hard. As I had never done a proper job in my life, I jumped at the opportunity. After all, it would only be for a couple of months. The job was great fun, and when I had swept the playgrounds in the morning at 9am, Jimmy allowed me to go home for my breakfast, where I would remain until just before mid-day. Mid afternoon Jimmy and I would be in the pub, where we would stay until just after 3pm, and then we would make our way back to put in a final appearance. I kept that job on and off for two years, and every time I returned from the continent I would work in the school.

Jimmy Rigby was on holiday and he left me in charge of the school. Well, I thought it was Christmas. It was in the middle of summer and my friend and I spent the evening in the Blue Angel Club in Liverpool City centre, a favoured spot for musicians to hang out after gigs. We were with two girls we had met at the club and my friend, Pete, suggested that we go to the school and have a cooling swim in the school swimming baths. We had been snorting cocaine and using other substances, and so we were oblivious to the fact that it was after four in the morning. As I could not swim (and still can't) I remained in the shallow end just to cool down from the intense heat. Suddenly, the doors burst open and the lights came on, and before we knew it several policemen with dogs surrounded us. We didn't know what to do and all just remained in the water, in our nude and totally shocked. I explained to the police that I was in charge of the school whilst the caretaker was away and just put myself at their mercy. I was certain we'd be arrested and I would be charged with abusing my position as the key holder of the school. After some dialogue between the policemen they agreed that no further action would be taken if I allowed them and their dogs to take a dip in the swimming pool. I was so relieved and agreed for them to do this. Afterwards, we locked up and made our way home. The following afternoon I was walking across the playground towards the main gate, when a voice boomed my name from the swimming bath's boiler room door. I turned to see Bill Johnson the swimming bath's attendant glaring at me and gesturing for me to come over.

He led me angrily through the swimming baths door and pointed at the water. 'What the bloody hell's this?' he bellowed. 'What's been going on?' The surface of the water was completely covered in dog fur, from one end of the bath to the other, just one blanket of furry mass. I knew Bill Johnson was fanatical about the water in the baths, and he was even meticulous about his boiler room, which he frequently cleaned and painted. I was speechless, and watched his fuming red face and bulging, angry eyes. He looked so funny and I just burst out laughing. I ran quickly from the baths and went to my hiding place at the top of the school. Needless to say, Bill Johnson reported me to the headmistress and I was severely reprimanded, with a serious threat of dismissal.

The final straw came when the oil for the boilers was delivered on the Monday morning. There were two oil pipes, one inlet for the heavy 950 oil, rather thick like diesel oil, and one for the paraffin oil that fuelled the water boiler. I wrongly assumed that the man who delivered the oil would know which was which, and so after unlocking the oil pipe cover, I went back into the school. I was talking to Dolly Mullen, one of the cleaners, when I heard an almighty commotion coming from outside in the street. The oil deliveryman stormed through the door, a complete look of anguish across his round pale face. 'I've put the oil in the wrong pipe' He shouted down the corridor. 'What will I do? I only started the job this morning.'

I couldn't believe it. But it was all entirely my fault. I was supposed to supervise oil deliveries and did not. The engineers were called out to strip the boilers and clean out the tanks. They were there until after midnight. However, although I was severely reprimanded yet again, I wasn't dismissed. I must say though that Jimmy Rigby, the caretaker was like a father to me, and was always making excuses for me and covering for me whenever I went missing, as was often the case. He was forever giving me fatherly lectures whenever I turned up for work in the morning, still out of my head from the night before. 'What are you doing to yourself, lad?' He'd say in his broad Liverpool voice. 'You've got your whole life ahead of you!' Needless to say, as much as I loved Jimmy, his words went in one ear and out of the other. He knew that, of course, and would just shake his head in exasperation.

CHAPTER ELEVEN
WITH A LITTLE HELP
FROM MY FRIENDS

The sixties and the so-called 'Flower Power' era was most certainly one of the most significant spiritual epochs in modern times. There was just something magical about that period that gave rise to many very sickly clichés such as 'Love, Peace and transcendental meditation', and also, 'Turn on, Tune in and drop out,' immortalised by the acid guru Timothy Leary. This period was probably the most exciting for me. Although I had formed a new band called Arnold Grenyard by this time, we had not played any gigs and so I was still 'between jobs', and just enjoying myself. It was a warm July Saturday evening and I was enjoying a drink with a friend in The Grosvenor Pub just down the road from my parent's house. It was quite crowded and I noticed a guy sitting opposite staring at me. He was quite portly with long thinning dark curly hair and a walrus moustache. In fact, he looked like Dave Crosby from Crosby Stills and Nash. I thought he looked quite cool as he sat there wearing shades and a huge grin. 'How's it goin' man?' he asked, rising from his chair to come and sit by my friend and I. 'I seem to know your face,' he went on. 'Do you live round here?'

'Sort of,' I replied. 'I've only just returned to Liverpool. I've been living in France.' We exchanged a few more pleasantries before I explained that I was in a band. My hair was down to my shoulders and I was looking quite gaunt and every bit the appearance of a musician in the sixties. He introduced himself as Tommy and said that he too had been living away and had only recently returned to Liverpool. One thing led to another and Tommy produced two small packages and held them in front of me. 'Have you tried Lyserg?' He grinned mischievously. 'Lysergic acid?' I stared at him blankly and felt my friend nudge me in the side.

'Acid, man.' Tommy went on. 'L.S.D. A Trip.' I felt my heart skip a beat and a rush of excitement pass through me. He unscrewed the silver paper from one of the packages to reveal two pieces of what looked like blotting paper. 'Here, put this on your tongue.' He was insistent and had a look of anticipation on his face, rather like a guru before the initiation of his devotee. I felt my friend prod me again as I carefully handled a piece of the paper and placed it on my tongue. 'I'm off!' said my friend. 'See you tomorrow.' Not wanting to get involved with the odd stranger, he left the pub.

After we'd finished our drinks we too left the pub. 'I'm going into town,' said Tommy. 'D'ya fancy coming?' I was wondering why I was still feeling quite normal and why nothing whatsoever had happened. I decided to go with him into town and together we made our way to the bus stop on Smithdown Road, the main route into the Liverpool City Centre. We'd walked no more than 50 yards when I was overcome with a strange sensation of disorientation. Although it was just after 10pm there was a strange light in the sky. Within 10 minutes the night had gone and it looked, to all intents and purposes, to be in the middle of the day. I was amazed to see a blue sky and the sun shining brightly. The main road looked like a mosaic pattern with different coloured flowers all along the pavement. It looked so surreal and rather like a Salvador Dali painting with me in the middle. Even though everything looked crazy, my senses were so intense, and I could hear and see very clearly. The ground beneath my feet suddenly felt like rubber and very springy, and at one point I felt if I jumped into the air I would not come back down to earth. One moment time appeared to stand still, and in the next it was like watching a cartoon movie that had been fast-forwarded with all the things around me passing very quickly by. Before I knew it the whole thing had stopped and we were both standing in a shop doorway at 4 in the morning, having gone nowhere. Of all the substances I had shoved into my body, this had truly been the most bizarre of all experiences, and most certainly one I was keen to replicate. As a direct result of this surreal experience Tommy and I became good friends. Unfortunately, though, it was a friendship that nearly brought about my ruination and ultimate demise.

In a very short space of time it was clear to me that I had become an addict in every sense of the word. I also began to rely on Tommy for everything, and then one day, for no apparent reason, he turned his back on me and walked away. That was it I was on my own. I had always survived and now I was more determined than ever. There was nothing else for it I had to get my new band on the road as soon as possible. Within weeks we were ready to take off to the continent again. We now I had a new name, a new style and only three of the original members. The band now consisted of our drummer, Paul Hitchmough, and the singer Steve Barton, and bass player Stevie Bowen, and myself. I had been contacted by an agent in France who expressed an interest in our new line-up. He came to the UK to see us and offered us a contract to tour the continent. It looked good to me, and that weekend we left once again for France. This time, though, we all had very long hair and had a repertoire of heavy rock and very progress music. Our agent, Christian had checked us into a small hotel above a cafe. It wasn't the most salubrious of places but at least it was clean and friendly. Besides, as Christian had booked us on to a fairly extensive tour, we'd be on the road most of the time so it was just somewhere to sleep at night. I had since found out from Steve Barton that my French son had been named Benjamin – Benjamin Favier – and that it might be possible for me to see him whilst I was in France. Although I did not relish the idea of meeting up with Marie Paul, the thought of seeing my son quite excited me.

When we arrived in France we were quite surprised to see that the music scene had dramatically changed. Our music was now regarded with some disdain and cynicism. There were very few people at our first gig, and the second wasn't very much better. We had been there for nearly a month with no sign of any money from Christian and a fairly large hotel bill to pay. In fact, Christian disappeared, and was never available when we phoned his office. It was clear that drastic measures were called for.

In the meantime Steve Barton took me to see baby Benjamin at Marie Paul's home. It was a very brief visit and I was not allowed to hold him. Marie Paul was at work and her mother stood guard over the baby, looking very much like a commandant in a concentration camp. She muttered something to me in French. 'You will never see him again.' Steve translated. 'That's it, Billy, let's go.' And as far as my son was concerned that was the only encounter I was to have – at least for some years.

We spent the following afternoon in our hotel room creating a plan. Paul came up with the crazy idea of lowering our cases out of the bedroom window to the street below. It was a mad idea but the only answer to the problem. We couldn't just walk out of the hotel as this meant passing the owner who also served in the café below. After drawing straws it was decided that Stevie Bowen, our new bass player, would stay in the room until the café below had closed. We had cut the sheets and blankets into strips and tied them tightly together so that we had a strong enough piece to lower our cases. Steve Barton had been staying with Monique, so Paul and I spent the night in a local bar. We remained there until we were certain it was safe to return to the hotel. The hotel was just around the border between France and Belgium on the French side. Any noise would alert the border guards, and so we had to be very quiet and just as careful. It was nearly 2am in the morning and you could have heard a pin drop. We parked just outside of the hotel and made sure the coast was clear. Paul whistled up to Steve who immediately began lowering the cases down to the street below. The building was two stories high and we had miscalculated the length of the blankets we had tied together. Although they only reached to approximately four feet above our heads we just about managed to grab hold of each case as they were lowered. We certainly underestimated my case – an Army travel trunk – and extremely large and heavy. In fact, it proved far too heavy for the tied blankets. We watched in horror as the blankets snapped and the heavy missile came hurtling down towards us, crashing on the pavement, and sounding, to all intents and purposes, like a mortar bomb in the Second World War. The impact resounded all along the narrow street, causing dogs to bark and lights to go on. The cobbled street was strewn with underpants, socks and shirts, which we bundled into the back of the van as fast as we could. The hotel manager was quickly alerted and Stevie Bowen made a hasty retreat as the elderly man was making his way along the corridor towards the stairs. We all breathed a sigh of relief as the van made its way round the corner towards the border. Paul handed the border guard our green card insurance only to be told it had expired at midnight. However, the young policeman appeared to be far more interested in the fact that we were an English band and ignored our expired insurance certificate. With a grin and an impressed look on his face, he said in perfect English, 'May I have your autographs?'

'Sure,' answered Paul, thinking that would be the end of the matter and he would then allow us to pass through the barrier. We all scribbled out signatures on the back of the scrap of paper he handed to us, and then he said, 'I'm sorry but I cannot allow you to go through.'

'But we've got to catch the ferry at Oustende,' retorted Paul excitedly. 'If we miss that one we'll be late for an important gig in London.' The young policeman was completely disinterested and shrugged his response.

Paul turned to me in search of a suggestion. I remembered I had some long playing records in my case and a pair of round gold-rimmed sunglasses just like the ones worn by John Lennon. The guard watched eagerly as I climbed into the back of the van to search my case. I retrieved the records and the sunglasses and handed them to the guard. His eyes suddenly widened, and clutching the gifts enthusiastically in his hands, he raised the barrier and waved us through. 'Goodbye,' he said smiling, a triumphant look on his face. 'Have a nice trip.'

Paul put his foot down and the van sped away as we all breathed simultaneous sighs of relief. Even though I was minus my sunglasses and Long Playing records, I was quite pleased and couldn't wait to get on the ferry and return to England.

It was quite a distance to Oustende, and even though Paul drove as fast as he possibly could we missed the ferry. This meant we'd have to wait until mid-day and take the risk of being arrested. Although we were all extremely tired we were unable to sleep. We waited anxiously for the mid-day ferry and then boarded it without a problem.

That was the last the continent would see of me as a musician, and I was only too glad to arrive safely home. Two weeks went by and my mother and father were in the living room talking and I was playing my guitar upstairs when someone came to the front door. My mother opened it to be confronted by two extremely tall and well-dressed men standing on the step. 'We are from Interpol,' one of the men announced producing his credentials. 'We have come to speak to William Roberts.'

My father joined my mother at the front door, and asked, 'What do you want him for?'

They explained that it was in connection with leaving a hotel without paying the bill and also for destroying the bedding.

'We would like him to come with us,' the other man continued.

'Do you have a warrant?' my father asked politely.

'No,' answered the man, 'we do not!'

'Then goodbye!' continued my father, closing the door in their faces.

Although my parents expected them to return with a warrant, we heard no more for a month. Then one morning I received an official looking document in the post from The Court of Lille. It said that I had been tried of fraud in my absence and found guilty. I had been fined over £200, with an order to pay within three months or serve a six-month prison sentence. This was quite a sum of money then, particularly to an out-of-work musician. I refused to pay the fine and did not hear another word about it. Of course, unless I wanted to spend some time in a French prison I couldn't set foot in France again – at least for a few years. In fact, it was nearly 25 years before I worked in France again.

CHAPTER TWELVE
NO TURNING BACK

People were already noticing that I had lost an awful lot of weight. I was 23 years old and just under 7 stones in weight. I was living with my parents and staying out all night. I'd lost interest now in music, and although I was still playing in local clubs, our band was nothing special and was just like a lot of other bands around at the time. Although I was addicted to a wide range of substances, I had to somehow keep it together if only for my parents' sake. If my father suspected anything at all to do with drugs, he would have given me the hiding of my life.

MY FATHER DIES

Everyone who knew my father knew only too well that he was a man of very few words. He was an extremely strong man who would say whatever was on his mind. Whenever he came home early my mother's friends would have to leave immediately. I suppose he was a chauvinistic man who believed that a woman's place was in the home. Even though my father was quite antisocial and very miserly, he loved animals and in fact had a way with them. He always said to me, 'Never trust anyone who doesn't like animals.' And this is something I've never forgotten.

My father was one of five children – four boys and one girl. My father's father, Edward William Walmsley Roberts was 46 when he married my grandmother, Jane Davies, when she was only 17. Together they ran a small but very well known pet shop at the back of the old St John's Market in the Liverpool City Centre. In fact, they owned the entire block, including a pub called the Duck House. Although my father was born in the pet shop, the family home was at 120 Penny Lane, of Beatles fame. From a very early age my father had an aptitude for buying and selling, and would make money from buying anything from antique furniture to cars and heavy goods wagons. However, the love of his life was the Fodens Steam Wagon. He had several of these and would travel all over the country with the haulage business he had set up. My dad became known for his passion for steam wagons, and it is still said today that there was nothing he didn't known about these coal-fuelled monstrosities of a bygone age. My mother told me that he frequently enlisted her help as his second man and stoker, when his friend had let him down and he had to transport a large delivery to Halifax or some other location. This accounts for the reason why my mother was strong and muscular and could turn her hand to anything. In fact, my father could also turn his hand to anything and very often did. He also dealt in scrap and dismantled two of the very last steam wagons in Liverpool. He gave the brass horns from the two steam wagons to an up and coming young comedian by the name of Ken Dodd, and the two brass coats of arms from the fronts of the wagons always hung in pride of place on the walls each side of the fireplace in our house. In fact, because my mother wanted the coats of arms to remain in the family, she left them in her will to my brother, Alby. She always maintained that he would keep them and that I would sell them to the highest bidder. Recently I was surprised to learn that my brother did sell my father's most precious items. All that I can say is that I definitely would have kept them, and felt more than a little let down by my mother. I recently met Ken Dodd after one of his shows and he was fascinated to learn that I was the son of Albert Roberts, the man who gave him the brass horns when he first started out as a young comedian. My father knew Ken Dodd's family well and would frequently take me to their place in Thomas Lane, Knotty Ash. The Dodd's had a huge yard where my father kept some of his vans and wagons. Ken Dodd's uncle was a dwarf and used to hide behind a rain barrel and pull faces at me. Ken was telling me that his uncle's diminutive figure was in fact the inspiration behind his famous Diddy Men. Everyone who knew him respected my father, and he was known all over Liverpool for his expertise of Steam Wagons and other steam driven machines.

It was 1970 and I was between bands again, the ever-popular excuse for an out of work musician in those days, but was playing temporarily with a band in and around Liverpool just to earn some money. It was Wednesday morning and I had just returned from the city centre to see my brother driving off with my mother and father. Aunt Sadie told me that dad was not too well and that my mother had made him go to the doctors. My father had never really been sick in his whole life and was not a fan of the doctors. I knew that if he had allowed my mother to take him to the doctors he must have really been feeling unwell. 'He's had pains in his stomach,' said Sadie. 'You know what your father is like, he just carries on.'

Over two hours later mum and dad returned from the doctors. It was the first time I'd really looked at my father closely, and I had to admit that he looked quite ill. He was grey and his eyes were sunken and heavy. My dad was a strong man and quite private. I don't think he shared his feelings with anyone and was most definitely a man who would not give in. I felt quite ashamed that I hadn't noticed just how ill he had looked for weeks. That's how wrapped up in my own little world I was at that time. He had to be cajoled into going to the doctors even though he was apparently in great pain. He returned home from the doctors and went straight to bed. The following day a specialist from Mossley Hill Hospital came with our GP to see him. He was immediately taken into hospital for exploratory surgery. I went in once to see him and then my mother asked me not to go in again. She said my hair was too long and the other patients were laughing and making my dad feel quite embarrassed. I immediately had it cut so I could visit him in hospital, but that very day he came home. His homecoming was perhaps the bleakest day of my life. The diagnosis cast a shadow on the entire house – my father had stomach cancer, which was inoperable. The prognosis was extremely bleak and one I did not want to face – he had weeks to live. I wanted so much to get close to him but had a feeling it was too late. His bed was brought downstairs to make him more comfortable and life much easier. He didn't sleep very well and would wake up around 5 every morning. I used to take him for a drive every morning in my 1952 Ford Anglia and we'd visit all his old 'haunts', the places that held some memory for him. The very last time I took him out he asked to be taken to Sefton Park Lake. In fact, that's the last memory I have of my dad on our morning trips out together. I will always have a memory of him standing on the steps and looking out over the Lake. It was a sunny May morning and it looked to me as though he was saying goodbye to everything he knew and loved. That afternoon my dad was cold so my mother lit a fire for him and then she went to do some shopping. My father sat in front of the fire with his hands cupped over the flames as he always did, then said, 'I won't see the summer, lad.'

'Don't be silly, dad,' I replied, not really knowing what to say. Deep down I knew he was right, and I also knew he wasn't afraid to die. He was more concerned about those he was leaving behind.

'You'll be alright, lad.' He added, with warmth in his voice that I'd never really heard before. My father never called me by my name. He either called me 'Babs' or 'Lad' and always expected me to respond. I didn't mind what he called me, why should I he was my dad. Watching him warming his hands over the fire made me feel sad. I hadn't really noticed before, but he had lost quite a lot of weight and had a look on his face that told me he had resigned himself to the cold fact that he was going to die.

Some time around 5am on the 16th May, my dad called my mother: 'I'm ready, Annie,' he said in a weak matter-of-fact voice. 'I need to go into hospital.'

The ambulance arrived within 20 minutes, and after my father was secured on a stretcher he was taken outside to the ambulance. I stood at the front door and watched with great sadness as my father asked the ambulance men to stop for a moment. He looked back at the house with a slight smile on his face and then gestured for the two men to carry on lifting him into the ambulance. The door was closed, and the vehicle carrying my dad pulled slowly away and took him from us forever.

I sat by the telephone in the living room playing my guitar and waiting for someone to call from the hospital. The call eventually came at 6.30. I immediately took my mother to the hospital to find that my father was in a deep coma and very close to death. My brother Alby later joined us, and he and my mother stood on one side of the bed, and I stood on the other. I'd never seen anyone die before and I felt afraid and so alone. 'He knows you're here,' my mother said to my brother, forgetting about me completely. It was like a knife to my heart. I kept saying to myself over and over again, 'Does he not know I'm here? Does he not know I'm here?' My mother obviously realised what she had said and looked across at me. 'He knows you're here as well.' The damage had already been done – I was devastated. I slid my hand beneath the sheets to feel my father's warm body. Although my dad's hands had always been huge and very hard, now they somehow felt soft and warm. Almost at that moment he made a strange sound – a rattle of some sort as though he was being sick. The nurses came and immediately covered his head with the sheet. My mother collapsed into my brother's arms and sobbed uncontrollably. They left the hospital and I drove to Sefton Park Lake to be alone. I've never cried so much in all my life. My father was dead. That strong man who had never been ill in his whole life had been destroyed by cancer, and I never told him that I loved him.

The following morning I was sitting in my father's chair playing my guitar. My mother had gone with my brother to make the funeral arrangements, and I was lost in thought. I saw something out of the corner of my eye, and swung my head round to see what it was. My father was standing in the doorway surrounded by a bright white light. He had that familiar half-smile across his lips, and although he didn't speak he nodded his goodbye and disappeared. 'Oh, dad,' I sobbed. 'I do love you.' I'd never told him that I loved him, and for that matter, he had never, ever told me. Now he had gone and I knew my life would change, and not necessarily for the better. My father held things together and kept me in control. What now?

They say there are skeletons in the cupboards of every family, and my family were most certainly no exception. I later learned that my mother and father had never been married, and that they only got married a couple of weeks before my father actually died. My brother, Alby, and his wife, Ethel, were the only other people present at the wedding, and I was not even told about it. I really could not forgive any of my family for depriving me of the opportunity of being at my parents wedding. More recently I have begun putting our family tree together and have again been hit with some more startling revelations about my family and who I really am. My mother had been married before and my brother had a different name on his birth certificate. It would seem that he wasn't really my big brother, Alby, after all, and the brother I looked up to as a child was not who I really thought he was. His name was not even Roberts. It's all too late now

– water under the bridge, as they say. Not for me though. When I was young I was always looked upon as being different from everyone else, a sort of freak with long hair and no ambition. Although I do admit that I frequently led a so-called 'heady' and carefree life, and spent most of my time out of my mind on drugs, it was quite usual for me to be criticised and wrongly accused by those who I really believed loved me. You do live and learn.

My father's death was a huge turning point in my life, the one catalyst that should have brought me to my senses, but sadly did the opposite. The one question I would love to ask my mother and father is 'Why didn't you tell me everything that I, as your son, had a right to know?'

Over the last few years I have in fact found more than one proverbial skeleton in the family cupboard. It would seem that my mother kept quite a few secrets from me, and although this does not stop me loving her, I can't help feeling more than a little angry with her.

CHAPTER THIRTEEN
BENEATH THE WINGS
OF ANGELS

I am quite sure it is the general consensus of opinion that mediums must be beyond reproach, and should never do anything wrong in their lives. I think I have always had a problem with this misconception, which is why I decided to write about everything I had done in my life. My mother always said 'When you tell everything about yourself nothing whatsoever can be said about you.' She was right and that is exactly why I have done just that.

After my father died my life seemed to spiral out of control. I spent my days completely out of it and never a day passed by when I wasn't under the influence of one narcotic substance or another. Although I was still living with my mother I was very rarely home. If I came home at all I would usually climb into bed around 5am and sleep till midday. My mother had always been slightly suspicious of me using drugs, but after my father died it became quite obvious. At the end of May 1970, I met a nurse called Penny. We'd been together for a month and, primarily because I felt quite trapped still living at home with my mother, we got married. The only people who knew that we'd got married were Steve Barton, the singer out of the Kru zads, and my friend, Tommy. I decided that I would still live with my mother, and not tell her that I'd got married until the time was right. It looked as though the time was never going to be right, and so Penny decided to tell my mother, regardless of what I thought. My mother could be a strong, volatile woman, and so initially she was quite angry, primarily because I hadn't waited very long after my father had died. Eventually, though, she helped us all she could, and Penny and I moved into 3 Lancaster Avenue, in the Sefton Park area. However, the marriage was quite explosive and, as a consequence, it came to an end in November of the same year. I do have to admit that it was my entire fault. Penny was only eighteen and I was 24. I used to take off to London without her for days, and expect everything to be back to normal on my return.

My brother Alby had two thriving engineering shops and my mother persuaded him to give me a little job, primarily to keep me occupied. This was probably the worst thing he could ever have done. After a short spell serving in one of his shops, it became clear to him that it was not for me. Rather than disappoint my mother he gave me a job driving one of his delivery vans. This was an ideal Job and meant that I was on the road every day away from everyone.

'I want you to collect a wagon engine from The Valley Service Station,' Alby demanded in his usual authoritative tone. 'Make sure the engine is secured before you leave the garage.'

The Valley Service Station was literally at the bottom of a steep incline. The engine had to be secured on blocks of wood and tied down with rope. I was slightly out of it that day – in fact, completely spaced out – and so I did not bother securing the engine before I moved off. I was driving quite fast up the steep hill and ignored the engine rocking from side to side. Half way up the hill there was a loud bang. I looked in the mirror and could see that the back doors of the van had burst open, and the engine had fallen onto the road and was rolling down the hill. Car horns sounded and I got the height of abuse from irate bus drivers and pedestrians, who'd narrowly missed colliding with the engine. Not knowing what to do, I found the nearest telephone and phoned my brother. He was there in ten minutes with some of the lads who worked in the shop. He went ballistic and threatened to put me back in the shop. My mother managed to talk him round, as she always did.

A few weeks later Alby announced that he was going on a trip to America. At that time I didn't have a car, and so my brother suspected that I would use the van at night for my own pleasure. He gave me strict instructions that at night the van must be returned to the garage. Of course, as the temptation was so great I had no intentions of doing that.

My brother and his family had been in America three days and I was taking the van home with me every night. I had been to a party with my friend Cliffy Jones in a tenement flat in Garston. We left the party around 3am and were driving along a very dark back street. I could only vaguely distinguish some road works ahead but because the oil storm lamps had been extinguished, I did not see the huge hole in the road. The inevitable and my worse nightmare happened – I drove the front end of my brother's orange van right into the hole. Luckily, Cliffy was a big guy and quite strong. Using all the strength he could find, he lifted the front of the van sufficiently for me to drive it on to solid ground. The bumper and front were all smashed in. I knew this would be the end where my brother and I were concerned. Cliffy managed to straighten the front sufficiently for us to drive home, but I was still faced with the problem of having it repaired before Alby returned home. My brother and I had a very strained relationship and he never needed much of an excuse to show his aggression towards me, and so it was vitally important that I had it repaired regardless of the cost. Luckily I knew enough people who would help me out. Alby Carmichael, a mutual friend of my brother and I, repaired the bodywork to its former glory, and I managed to match the paint to have it sprayed. It was perfect and my brother never found out until I told him recently.

Ever since I was a child I had always had a strong feeling that I was being looked after and living my life beneath the wings of angels. Although my drug abuse appeared to somehow cloud my judgement and suppress my psychic skills, my senses we enhanced sufficiently for me to know that I would always be looked after. It seemed that whenever I was in trouble someone or something always came to my rescue.

Working at my brother's shop meant that I could save enough money to buy a car – a Ford Cortina GT. This was my pride and joy and gave me my freedom once again. It didn't matter to me that I would always be under the influence of something; I just needed wheels to get out and about.

By now my life was hell and I needed something everyday to get me through. It was now New Year's Eve 1972 and I was 26 years old. I had sold all my guitars and sound equipment just to feed my growing habit. To me I was on a mission and trying desperately to achieve something, to everyone else I was on a self-destruct course. I had gone to Dutch Eddy's, a club situated in Parliament Street, in the Toxteth area of Liverpool, with my friend Cliffy and another guy and his girlfriend. Cliffy and I had a party to go to and were trying to find an excuse to get away from the other two. It was 11.40 and we had to leave. Unable to find the right excuse, we had to bring them with us. We had reached Upper Parliament Street, the continuation of Parliament Street, and were driving about 50 miles an hour. The traffic lights suddenly changed and I put my foot hard on the brake. The car shuddered and seemed to turn a 100 degrees and then lifted into the air. That's all I remember. I hadn't been wearing a seatbelt and when I regained consciousness I was somehow half on the bonnet of the car and the steering wheel had buckled. Cliffy had been thrown from the car and was picking himself up from the pavement, and the other guy and his girlfriend were unconsciousness in the back of the car, covered in blood. Within moments the ambulance and police had arrived, I lost consciousness again and woke up in hospital. The police were desperate to breathalyse me and take a blood test. Luckily for me because I was in hospital it was not allowed. I had sustained a fractured skull and some glass in my eye. Unfortunately though my car was a write off and because I only had third party fire and theft I received nothing from the insurers. The remains of my car went to a salvage yard for the princely sum of £50, but I still had to pay what was owing on the finance. The two passengers in the back of the car received considerable compensation for their extensive injuries, but my old friend Cliffy refused to make a claim. As a direct consequence of the accident I didn't drive for three years.

STEPS UP TO THE CHURCH

For a while my drug consumption increased and I found myself in a veritable psychological and emotional mire. I felt lost and just wanted to die. I was still living at my mother's house and she was continually threatening me with my brother every time I stepped out of line. Unbeknown to anyone I decided that I had to end my life. It got so bad for me that I dreaded getting out of bed in the morning for fear what the day was going to bring. I don't think I've ever been as sad and depressed as I was then, and I had absolutely nobody with whom to share my sadness. The only thing I had to decide was how I was going to kill myself. I wandered through the streets in a complete haze and found myself at the gates of a church not far from my mother's home. A lady had just come out so I knew it was open. I needed some solace and just wanted to sit quietly before I finally decided on anything drastic. The church was empty and my steps echoed from wall to wall as I walked slowly towards the altar. I sat quietly in front of a large figure of St Teresa of the Roses, my favourite Saint. I was suddenly overwhelmed with emotion and could not hold back the tears. I buried my head in my hands and sobbed uncontrollably when I heard a soft

Irish voice say, 'Can I be of any help my son?' I quickly looked up to see a tall and quite elderly grey haired priest standing over me. Before I could say a word he sat down on the pew beside me. He had an extremely kind manner and exuded a sense of peace and serenity. I felt quite comfortable with him, and he listened intently as I told him the whole story from beginning to end. When I had finished, he looked at me with large blue eyes full of compassion. 'Well,' he said thoughtfully, 'I think your troubles ended with the steps up to the church, don't you?' He rose slowly to his feet, smiled and made the sign of the cross in front of me. 'God bless you my son.' He turned and then made his way down the aisle towards the church door. I looked at St Teresa for a moment then turned to see the elderly priest, but he had gone! He had disappeared without trace. The church fell once again into silence, and I somehow felt so much better for having spoken to the elderly priest.

Some months later I returned to the church primarily to thank the elderly priest for listening to me and offering words of encouragement. Presuming that he lived in the house next to the church, I walked up the path towards the front door, and before I could even ring the bell, the housekeeper opened the door, and then proceeded to polish the brass knocker. I explained that I had come to see the elderly Irish priest. The woman had a puzzled look across her face as though she didn't know who I was talking about. 'Well,' she said, 'the priest here is only young, and he's not Irish. I've been housekeeper for over twenty years.' She could see the disappointment on my face as I turned to walk away. 'Just a minute,' she said, turning to go back into the house. Within seconds she returned with a framed monochrome photograph and held it in front of me. 'Is this the priest?' My eyes lit up and I nodded, 'Yes, that's him.' The woman lowered the photograph and smiled warmly. 'That's father McIntyre,' she said quietly. 'He's been dead now for fifteen years. He was a good man, and you're not the first to have seen him, and I'm certain you won't be the last.' Although I had always been used to seeing 'dead' people, this man had appeared to me as solid and substantial as the woman standing before me. I couldn't believe it. I bade the housekeeper farewell and then turned and made my way back along the narrow pathway towards the gate, turning for a moment to glance at the church next door. The priest was right - my troubles had ended with the steps up to the church. Sadly, like every other church today, because of the growing vandalism its doors are no longer open.

Even in my darkest hour I have always felt as though I was living my life beneath the wings of angels – always knew I was being watched and looked after. My experience with the Irish priest was a prime example. Although this did not deter me from using drugs, it did make me change my mind about ending my own life, and was also a huge turning point in my life.

CHAPTER FOURTEEN
THE BEGINNING OF
THE END

By now I had enough awareness of my life to know that it had spiralled completely out of control. I had been in and out of hospital with numerous drug overdoses, and each day was a struggle and presented me with innumerable seemingly insurmountable problems. If you have ever woken up the morning after a heavy party, and not remembered what had happened the night before, you will have a pretty good idea what I am talking about. The only difference with my amnesia was that I couldn't remember the last few years. The only friend I now had left was Cliffy Jones, and apart from him it seemed that I was completely alone. I could not see a way forward, and the only thing I had for support were the drugs I shoved into my body. It may sound a little strange but some days it sufficed just to know that I had stuff to use, and so this gave me a high in itself.

A HELPING HAND

It was sometime in the early seventies and I was now living in a one bedroom flat in Sydenham Avenue in the Sefton Park area of Liverpool. I was with my oldest friend Cliffy Jones and we were making our way home after a night in the famous Blue Angel Club in the Liverpool city centre. It was the early hours of Sunday morning, and we were both under the influence of cocaine and Strawberry Fields, an LSD derivative. We were both extremely spaced out and completely out of control. Although I was quite used to this state of mind, it was all new to Cliffy and he was falling all over the road laughing uncontrollably. Luckily there was no one around and so I just left him. We eventually reached the Zebra crossing outside of Sefton General Hospital, and I noticed three guys and their girlfriends on the opposite side of the road. As Cliffy and I began stumbling our way across the Zebra Crossing, they too decided to cross from the opposite side of the road. When they were almost in front of us, one of the guys sudden turned and head butted Cliffy, and he fell heavily to the ground laughing. I was speechless and everything seemed to happen in slow motion. A second guy punched me in the face and, although I did not feel the impact of his fist against my cheek, my head was thrown so far back that it made contact with the tarmac, splitting the back of my head wide open. Although my head felt extremely wet I didn't feel anything at all and, judging by Cliffy's laughter, neither did he. I decided to stay down on the ground until our attackers had gone. However, Cliffy's laughter angered them even more and they decided not to let it rest there. Walking back to us, one of the guys pulled an extremely long and shiny knife from inside his jacket, and then began making his way fiercely towards me. His friends were goading him by calling in unison 'Give it to him'. They kept on chanting until the anger showed on his face and he lunged towards me in a fit of rage. Even though I was completely out of it, I could see that this guy was off his head and was serious about doing me some harm. As I rolled over onto my side, to avoid the thrust of his knife, I heard some different, aggressive voices coming from behind me. There was a little commotion, and then I felt someone roughly grab hold of me. As I was completely out of it, I was only vaguely aware of being lifted from the ground and carried across the road. I was eventually deposited into the front garden of a funeral parlour, and felt myself passing through a privet hedge to land heavily on the concrete path leading to the front door. 'Stay there!' the voce called. 'Don't move!'

There was more commotion followed by sudden silence. I

lay there quite still for some time, and then I braved an eye through the privet hedge to check what exactly was happening. Cliffy was already standing up talking to two guys. He saw me and then called me over. Our rescuers stood there grinning triumphantly whilst our attackers had obviously fled. Still slightly coherent, and somewhat confused, I was relieved that the ordeal was finally over. I could feel my heart pounding inside my chest and the nerves all over my body tingling. Cliffy began falling about and laughing again. Although completely out of focus, our two rescuers introduced themselves. 'Billy,' one grinned, 'it's me, Billy Coyne.'

I paused for a few moments to think about what I was going to say.

'Billy,' I mumbled incoherently, 'How...'

I had known Billy Coyne since he was a young boy and I was best man at his brother's wedding, in the early sixties. I couldn't believe that he was one of our rescuers. The other guy introduced himself as Danny McCarthy, also someone I had known since I was very young. The whole thing was quite bizarre and far more than a coincidence. As it turned out, Billy Coyne lived in Portman Heights, a block of flats overlooking the Zebra Crossing where the incident had taken place. Upon hearing the commotion, they had looked through the window and seen Cliffy and me being attacked.

This was just another example of exactly how I was guided by angels. In fact, I have always said that 'something always comes up'. When I am in a difficult situation – I have always been saved at the last minute! I do hope that this continues to be the case.

Within the last few years, my oldest friend, Cliffy Jones, died of cancer. I had known Cliffy since we were babies, and although I was two years older than him, he was always protective towards me. Cliffy faced the end of his life courageously and with dignity. In fact, I have never seen anyone die so bravely. If he was afraid of dying he certainly did not show it. I visited him every day and was with him an hour or so before he died.

Although I've got an extremely strong constitution, I really did feel as though I was near the end of my life. It was 1974 and I was staying at my mother's house. She had gone out for the night with my aunt Sadie, and I had taken a large amount of an amphetamine based substance and a few lines of cocaine. I must have been quite run down at this point and not feeling too well, because instead of the usual chemical rush, I couldn't breathe and my heart began beating so fast that I was sure it was going to burst. The next thing I remember I woke up in a hospital bed on a drip. They told me I'd had a massive overdose, and because I'd been hospitalised so many times with overdoses, I was admitted to the psychiatric wing for assessment. This was probably one of the most horrific experiences of my life, and one I shall never forget. Whilst in the ward I was visited by a young psychiatrist by the name of Latandre, a very quiet and gentle guy in his mid-thirties. He was the first medical person who had taken the time to treat me like an intelligent human being, and although he told me in no uncertain terms that I would soon die if I continued on the road I was on, (the last thing I wanted to hear,) it really did bring me quickly to my senses. I listened to Dr Latandre and really took notice of what he was saying. He told me that my blood pressure was quite high and that he would come and discharge me the following day, as long as everything was back to normal. However, the following morning I got myself ready only to be told by one of the nurses that I was being kept in for observation for a few weeks at least. 'No way!' I thought. 'I'm not staying in this madhouse!' As all the windows on this particular ward only opened a fraction, 'a security measure!' I bided my time until one of the nurses was smoking outside the fire door. Once his back was turned I snuck quietly past him and ran as fast as I could through the hospital grounds. Needless to say my mother was not very pleased to see me; she went ballistic and, as always, threatened to phone my brother to take me back to the hospital.

From then on I decided that something had to be done about my life. I began having more and more psychic flashes, and knew then that the abilities I'd had since I was a child were obviously coming back with a vengeance. It may sound a little far-fetched, but it suddenly felt as though there was a supernatural force taking control of my life. I had always been clairaudient and clairvoyant, and because of my psychological state, I was beginning to think that the voices I was hearing were symptoms of some sort of mental illness. I really did think I was losing my mind, and didn't know what to do, or where to turn. I received very little medication to aid my withdrawal from drugs, and in those days the support left a lot to be desired. I continued to see a psychiatrist, and was extremely determined to break free of the chemical substances that had ruled my life for so long. Although my mother gave me a lot of support, she did not really understand what was happening to me and the trauma I was experiencing. I'd spent a veritable lifetime completely out of my mind, and now I was out in the cold and left to my own devices. I always remember what Bob Hope said when he gave up drinking, 'This is the best I'm going to feel all day!' That was exactly it! I did not know what to do with myself.

My mother was book keeping for my brother and had just returned home. It was a brisk November's afternoon, and I had decided to take my dog Lucky for a walk. I turned the corner from Grosvenor Road into Ash Grove and had reached the waste ground where prefabs used to be. I suppose I had been down Ash Grove a million times over the years, but this time I looked at the empty space with complete horror as though I was looking at it for the first time. They'd already begun erecting new house, but now it was possible to

Ivor James' sketch of Tall Pine

Billy and French son Benjamin

18 year old Billy, just returned from Continent

Billy (back left) and his band,
Belguim, 1965

Billy's Mum and Dad, 1948

Billy with actress friend, Eithne Browne,
at a book signing, 2008

Billy filming *Ghost Files* with celebrity friends 1995

Billy and Ken Dodd after a show, 2006

Billy filming *Ghost Hunter* in haunted graveyard in Louisiana swamps

Billy (far right) with *The Rolling Stones* after a gig

Billy with exorcist monk on Maltese television, 2001

Kiki Dee and Billy after one of his seminars, 1995

Billy's mum and aunt Sadie
in the late 50s

2 year old Billy in hospital.
Ghostly face above his head!

Billy filming Ghost Hunter in
the Haunted Plantation House
in New Orleans

Above: Billy's friend,
medium Doris Stokes,
in hospital before she died

Right: Billy and wife, Dolly,
in Torquay, 2005

actually see straight through from Ash Grove to Wavertree Vale. I suddenly felt overwhelmed with a strange feeling. My heart began to pound and my legs felt like jelly. If you've ever found yourself in an extremely terrifying situation, then I think you'll know exactly what I mean! However, I was terrified for no particular reason. My hands went rigid, as though I had cramp in them, and I had a tight band across my chest, as though I was having a heart attack. That's all I can recall. The next thing I knew I was banging frantically on my mother's front door, unable to breathe and shaking from head to toe. As soon as the front door had been opened, I quickly pushed passed my mother and ran as fast as I could down the narrow hallway and into the living room. Once in the safety of my home the panic and sheer terror just disappeared. Although quite exhausted, I felt quite relaxed and normal. 'Where's Lucky?' My mother said anxiously. 'Where's my baby?'

'In Ash Grove!' I stuttered incoherently. 'I left him down the road.'

Without even asking me what was wrong, she immediately went to find our loving, little Border Collie, Lucky. He had been sitting obediently exactly where I had abandoned him, waiting patiently to be collected.

I dreaded the horrific experience being repeated, and so I would not set foot over the doorstep. When I eventually did, the same thing happened again.

After undergoing even more psychotherapy, it was concluded that my nervous system had been so traumatised that now I was suffering from the debilitating condition called Agoraphobia, the fear of open spaces. The only problem was I also began to experience the same panic whilst remaining in my home. My life was totally miserable, and for me it was like living in hell. I wanted desperately to run away but I knew that there was nowhere to go. Like it or not, I had to face the problem somehow or other.

I was sent back to the rehabilitation centre in which I had originally been treated, and remained there for three months. Because I had abused all sorts of drugs for the best part of twelve years, it was decided that it was best to avoid any sort of medication. I had studied meditation in the sixties (nearly everyone did,) and so I decided that this process of mental discipline was the best approach. Based on a yogic form of meditation, using breathing and concentration, I created my own technique of meditation. It was not easy, but thank God, it worked.

When I had overcome all that, I began coughing copious amounts of blood, a symptom of Bronchiectasis. I became really ill and my weight decreased even more.

CHAPTER FIFTEEN
NOT ALL ANGELS
HAVE WINGS...

It's funny, but when you've lost everything and you are at an extremely low ebb, nobody seems to want to know. By now I was so weak and feeling very ill, that I got up in the morning and just sat all day in front of the television. There I remained until it was time to go to bed. The following day, the same process was repeated. In fact, one day was much the same as the other, and for me life was a complete misery. The hospital had exhausted all different types of antibiotics, and so they decided it was best for me to rest at home. I really was on the point of death, and just waited for the moment to come.

It was Monday afternoon and there was a programme on the television called Good Afternoon. It was the profile of a Harley Street Spiritual Healer by the name of Ted Fricker. I listened with interest, and at the conclusion of the programme they gave the address of The National Federation of Spiritual Healers. Although virtually too weak to move, I somehow found myself sitting up with a piece of paper and pen in my hand. I scribbled the address down, and my mother posted it for me the following day. Within no more than three days I received a visitor from the NFSH. He introduced himself as Des Tierney, and although at first my mother wasn't going to invite him in, she decided that he might just be able to help me.

Meeting Des Tierney was probably one of the best things that had happened. He gave me Spiritual Healing, and would visit me nearly every day. He was also a hypnotherapist and treated me with this of a weekend. More than this though, Des Tierney was a mine of information and gave me the right books to read. We became good friends and I will always be grateful for his help, time and patience.

BUZ KASHI

I was now beginning to feel that the Spirit World had well and truly begun to come back into my life. I had been clairaudient since I was a child, and although this had been slightly suppressed over the years, it was now beginning to manifest again. The main communicator, as always, was Tall Pine. I was still very vulnerable and wasn't really sure that I was really ready.

It was a pleasant sunny afternoon and I was relaxing in front of the television watching the horseracing from Newmarket. By this time I only had five pounds in my pocket and suddenly had what I thought was an incredible idea. Saint Paul had once said, 'Test the Spirits,' and test them I had decided to do. I said, in no uncertain terms, 'If you are not a figment of my imagination, give me the name of a horse that will win?' Although there was no response at that time, later on in the afternoon I heard someone say 'Buz Kashi.' I sat bolt upright in my chair and asked for it to be repeated. 'Buz Kashi,' the voice said again. I quickly grabbed the newspaper and flicked excitedly through the racing pages. I couldn't find any horse with that name. It was on my mind all night, and the following morning I scanned the horse index at the back of the paper and could not believe it. There it was, BUZ KASHI. I checked it and double checked it and it was in the 2.30 at Newmarket. It was running at 33/1 and it was owned by the Agha Kahn. I put what money I had on the horse at the local betting shop and returned home to watch it win still at 33 to 1. 'Thank you Tall Pine,' I said dancing round the room. 'Now I know you are not a figment of my imagination. Thank you.' However, disappointment came when I went to collect my winners later that afternoon.

Buz Kashi had been disqualified for interfering with another horse. That was a lesson learned. I asked for a winning horse to prove that Tall Pine was real but I was not allowed to make money from it. This was in fact the first of many pieces of evidence to prove to me that I was being guided by unseen angelic forces. As Saint Paul had suggested in Corinthians, I tested the Spirit, and the incident with Buz Kashi proved once and for all that 'they' were close to me. Although I did not win any money I did feel extremely comforted by the very fact the horse they had given did win even though it was disqualified. Incidentally, I never saw Buz Kashi in the racing pages again after that, nor did I ever try to use my psychic powers to win money ever again. That was a lesson well learned.

SPIRITUALISM

Gradually my health improved and my life got better. Then, early one evening the phone rang and my mother answered it. It was my mother's sister, Louise. She had always been the eccentric one in my mother's family. 'They told me he's ready now!' she blurted down the phone. 'Can I speak to him?'

My mother raised her brows, and then rolled her eyes heavenward as she handed me the phone. 'It's aunty Lou!'

'I want you to come with me to Allerton Spiritualist Church tomorrow night!' she insisted, 'I'll meet you there. It's above The Dudley Institute.'

That was my introduction to the religion of Spiritualism. I sat quietly in the very small congregation with my aunty Louise. I watched nervously as the elderly lady medium sat directly in front of us. I couldn't take my eyes of her, and once the prayer had been said, and hymns sung, this diminutive, and very quietly spoken lady began passing on messages from the Spirit World to selective members of the congregation. When she pointed to me I nearly died. 'Your father, Albert, is saying you've finally done it, lad, now be

91

strong! You have much work to do for the Spirit World, and so you must prepare yourself.' That was it! I was completely mesmerised. She even knew my father's name. I looked sideways at my aunty Louise, and she had a slight grin of achievement across her lips and her eyes were closed. I was suspicious, and wondered if she told the medium my father's name. She later assured me that she hadn't, and I did believe her. I went to the Allerton Spiritualist Church the following Tuesday and was amongst those selected to sit in a so-called 'development' circle. Although I had been psychic since I was a child, I was told that sitting in such a circle under the supervision of an experienced medium, would help to refine and channel my skills. I was surprised to find the diminutive, elderly medium who had given the message that first night in the Spiritualist Church, was to run the circle. I now felt a little more relaxed and began to look forward to the whole experience.

TALL PINE MAKES HIS PRESENCE FELT

As the weeks went by, Miss Alexio, as she was affectionately called, decided that a few of the 'sitters' were unsuitable, and so she politely asked them to leave. Once the circle was settled, Tall Pine began to overshadow me and, although at the time I had been completely oblivious to the fact, later I learned that his philosophical words of wisdom had been had been spoken through me. To be quite honest, I was a little unnerved by the very thought of this, and some weeks I would make an excuse and just not go. I know this was not the polite thing to do, particularly that Miss Alexio had taken me under her wing, but I was beginning to wonder if this was what I wanted to do! However, each time I missed, precisely at 9.45, the phone would ring. The pips would go and a few moments silence would ensue. 'Sylvia speaking,' the frail voice would say at the other end of the phone. 'Why didn't you attend tonight?'

Miss Alexio could see right through my feeble excuses, and so I decided to persevere and attend religiously each week.

I sat in Sylvia Alexio's circle for four years, and must say her humility, knowledge and understanding of the Spirit World taught me a great deal about myself and my own mediumistic skills. It was now 1981 and I had met Annie Yaffe, the daughter of a very well known healer, Helen Yaffe. Annie and I got married in 1982, and on May 3rd 1983, my son, Benjamin Jacob was born. I can already hear you saying to yourself, 'but haven't you got a French son called Benjamin?' This was another one of those very weird coincidences that have taken place in my very unusual life. Benjamin Jacob was named after Annie's father, (deceased,) and so I had nothing whatsoever to do with the choosing of his name. Nor did I have anything to do with choosing my French son's name. Coincidence, or what?

By this time I had taken time out of the circle, just until things had settled down with the newly born Ben. We were driving home one afternoon when there was a news announcement about a fire in which an elderly lady had been badly burned and was in a critical state in hospital. I later learned from my mother that the elderly lady was in fact Sylvia Alexio. I just couldn't believe that this gentle and very spiritual lady could have been subjected to such a horrible accident. Miss Alexio lived in a one bedroom flat and had been smoking in bed and had fallen asleep. When we went to see her in hospital she was unrecognisable and in a semi-conscious state. Whilst I stood at her bedside, Miss Alexio braved an eye open and mumbled to me, 'Tell your tall friend to come further into the room.'

'I'm alone, Miss Alexio,' I said, turning to look at the door. Tall Pine was standing there, solemn faced and arms folded across his chest. I then knew she was not going to make it. In fact she died a couple of hours later.

All the time I had sat in Sylvia Alexio's circle, she had made every endeavour to get me to accompany on the Spiritualist platform. 'Just to allow Tall Pine to say a few words,' she would always say. Of course, I always declined, making some silly excuse. It was at her funeral that Eddie Emmery, another Liverpool veteran medium, (now deceased,) persuaded me to accompany him during one of his services, at The Psychic Truth Society, another local Spiritual Church. 'I'll give the clairvoyance and you give a short talk,' he said, with some determination. I reluctantly agreed, but after all I was in safe hands. He was an old hand at it, and I felt sure he would give me all the support I needed. However, at the very last moment Eddie phoned me to say that he had double-booked, and said that I would have to take the whole service by myself. I did, and that was the beginning of my career as a Spiritualist medium. The service went quite well, I thought, and that night I climbed exhausted into bed. I had an extremely vivid and very lucid dream that the phone was ringing beside my bed, and when I answered it I could hear the familiar beeps of the payphone. 'Sylvia speaking!' said the gentle voice of Miss Alexio. 'I'm very pleased!' and then the line went dead and woke with a start. I lay there for a few moments, a contented smile across my lips, before snuggling down beneath the warm sheets. I now knew that Sylvia Alexio was pleased and obviously watching over me. She was alright now, and had gone home. My work as a Spiritualist medium was about to begin.

CHAPTER SIXTEEN
TALL PINE

Ever since I can remember I had always had a close association with Tall Pine, or TP as he is affectionately known. To me he was and still is as solid and tangible as any other living person, and although he never really spoke to me, we did have an extremely fluent telepathic relationship. When I was a baby my mother used the branch of a tree as a mobile, which she would tie to the handle of my pram for me to watch. The motion and sound of the leaves moving in the wind would somehow lull me to sleep and give me a great deal of comfort. Looking back I am sure that this had something to do with Tall Pine. My mother was the only other person who had been aware of TP, and although he would communicate with me telepathically, I would frequently be heard talking, seemingly to myself.

When I began to seriously investigate Spiritualism, I had a private consultation with a very well-known Scottish medium by the name of Mary Duffy, (now deceased.) Nobody except me knew Tall Pine's name, and so I was quite surprised when, during the half hour consultation, Mary said, 'Tall Pine is here! He is telling me to tell you that if you get the opportunity to have a consultation with a 'good' psychic artist, he will make certain you get a drawing of him.' If this were true it would be amazing. Some time later on the recommendation of veteran Spiritualist, Gladys Owen, I booked an appointment with visiting world-renowned psychic artist, Ivor James. At that time I had no idea what to expect. I'd never met Ivor James before, and he most certainly knew nothing whatsoever about me. He was from Cambridgeshire and travelled all over the world. I nervously entered the room above Daulby Street Spiritualist church, and then sat carefully on the chair opposite Ivor. He was already sketching, and the sound of his pencil scratching across the surface of the paper seemed to echo across the room. 'You know who I'm drawing, don't you?' He said, peering over the top of his glasses to look at me.

'I think so!' I stuttered clumsily. 'I mean, I hope so!' At that moment all my faith was in the tip of Ivor's pencil, and my future work solely depended on the sketch he was going to produce for me. I could feel my heart racing inside my chest, and that moment time seemed to stand still. It took no longer than fifteen minutes for him to complete the drawing, at which time, he sprayed a fixer across the paper, inspected his work for a few seconds, and then turned it to face me. I gasped in disbelief. 'TALL PINE!' I exclaimed. 'That's Tall Pine!'

'I know!' Ivor James mumbled, coughing quietly to clear his throat. 'Who else would it be?'

I thanked him, and left the room feeling as though I was floating on cloud nine. I was so excited, and couldn't wait to get home to show my mother the sketch of Tall Pine. This still hangs with pride in my study at home. Ivor James and his wife, Marjory became good friends. Ivor worked frequently at my centre in Liverpool, and would nearly always only take travelling expenses, and never a fee.

CHAPTER SEVENTEEN
MY WORK AS A MEDIUM
REALLY BEGINS

Although my English son, Benjamin Jacob was to be brought up in the Jewish faith, he was named, (the Spiritualist form of Christening) by the famous Scottish medium, Mary Duffy (now deceased,) at The Psychic Truth Society, and was given the Spirit name of 'David'. Shortly after he was named I received an invitation from Nora Moore, the national president of the Greater World Christian Spiritualist Association to give the address at the very prestigious Anniversary Meeting held annually at Leeds Town Hall. There was an expected audience of 2000 people, and I was to be accompanied on the stage by medium Doreen Lewis (now deceased.) In the early days I never quite knew what exactly to expect when standing before a large audience. After all, I was at the mercy of Tall Pine; without him I was nothing. Tall Pine spoke through me for half an hour, and the day was concluded with an impressive demonstration of mediumship from Doreen Lewis. The day went so well that Doreen and I were invited to appear at the Greater World's London Anniversary, to be held at the Friend's Meeting House in Euston Road, London. I was very proud and so excited. In those days I still had long hair and always appeared in tatty jeans and white baseball pumps. I had gone along to see the president of The Psychic Truth Society and was asked to wait outside the mediums room where there was a committee meeting taking place. As the dialogue was fairly heated I couldn't help hearing what was being said. Suddenly, to my great disappointment, my name was mentioned. 'How could The Greater World ask someone like him to represent them at the Anniversary again in London?' I heard the church's president, Mabel Robertson say. 'He's got long hair and always wears jeans.' I had thought Mabel Robertson liked me and I was quite saddened by what I had heard. She was quite shocked to see me waiting outside the room and knew that I had obviously heard everything. 'I thought it's what's in the heart that matters?' I said, shaking my head as I walked from the church, feeling totally let down and quite disgusted. This was the first of many eye-openers for me where Spiritualism was concerned, and most certainly one that prepared me for all the jealousy and backbiting amongst Spiritualists. Unfortunately, it was this episode in my life that made me very radical, cynical and arrogant, ultimately turning a lot of people against me.

A LESSON LEARNED

When I was preparing for the event in London I wasn't really sure how to travel. It was suggested that because I was going to be extremely nervous it would be a good idea to travel by train. At least that way I could relax and be refreshed when I arrived in London. When I arrived at Lime Street Station it was announced that because of a collision all trains to London had been diverted. This meant I would arrive in London two hours before the event at 1.30, still giving me plenty of time to prepare. However, disaster struck! The train I was travelling on broke down just outside of Crewe and remained incapacitated for over fours hours. I arrived in London totally exhausted and three hours late for the meeting. I missed everything. When I returned home to Liverpool I decided to call to see my mother. I had only driven my car 20 yards when there was a loud noise from the engine and the car stopped in a cloud of black smoke. The engine had packed up, making me realise that all routes to London had been barred. This was a stern warning to the arrogant Billy Roberts who had become too complacent about his work. The Spirit World was not going to allow this to happen and had prevented me from appearing at one of the most important events in Spiritualism. Tall Pine was disgusted with me and said that I had to change.

THE THOUGHT WORKSHOP IS BORN

Although at this point I was still serving Spiritualist churches throughout the United Kin gdom, I was disillusioned and totally fed up with the politics of Spiritualism. As a direct result of my outspoken attitude I had acquired more enemies than friends and was finding it very difficult to do my work in the way I thought it had to be done. Spiritualism desperately needed to be modernised and brought in to the twentieth century. This was a change that was resented by the diehard Spiritualists who had made Spiritualism archaic and very cliquey. Against great opposition I established The Thought Workshop, the northwest's first centre for psychic and spiritual studies and alternative therapies. This was opened in Rodney Street, the Harley Street of Liverpool, supported by the Psychic News and visited by some of the best-known mediums in the country. Although the SNU, (The Spiritualist' National Union) greatly objected to what I was trying to do, The Greater World supported me all through. Although the SNU tried to prevent its registered mediums from working at The Thought Workshop, most of them ignored the hierarchy and still came to work there. It was through The Thought Workshop that I became friends with some of the veterans of Spiritualism. Ivor James, world renowned Psychic Artist did more for me personally than any other medium, and frequently refused to take a fee or even expenses for the work he did at the centre. Other famous mediums that worked at the centre were Ursula Roberts, medium to Ramadan and spiritual teacher and the author of many books on the subject. Sadly, like Ivor James, Ursula passed away some years ago. Others who worked there were

Eileen Roberts long time president of the ISM, Queenie Nixon (transfiguration medium), Don Galloway medium and Spiritual teacher; Ray Williamson the veteran medium, and Ray Williams, transfiguration medium. We also had homoeopathists, Reflexologists, Spiritual Healers, Reiki Healers, Dieticians, parapsychologists, mediums and clairvoyants, and many others. The centre was open from 10am until 10pm, seven days a week. The Psychic News arranged for the great medium Doris Stokes to do the official opening of the centre. As most people know Doris Stokes was a world famous medium and author of many best selling books. In fact, it was Doris who offered me the most encouragement regarding my work. She agreed to do the official opening of my centre, and she used to phone me every couple of days or so just to have a chat. During one of our long telephone conversations Doris blurted 'Albert – your father is telling me he is proud of you.' Doris did not know anything whatsoever about my family, and most certainly did not know my father's name. 'He's telling you to keep on going – everything will be alright.' Doris paused for a few moments. 'Who's Annie?' she asked.

'My mother,' I replied.

'He's sending his love to her.' She fell silent again. 'The funny thing is, my love, he's not calling you Billy. He keeps referring to you as Lad.'

'I understand, Doris,' I acknowledged. 'My father never, ever called me by my name. Up until the age of 16 he called me Babs. After that, right up until the day he died in 1970, he called me Lad.'

'Got to go now, dear,' Doris said. 'There's someone at the door.' Then, as always during my conversations with Doris, the phone went silent. Doris's manager, Laurie O'Leary then invited me to present one of her last shows at the Crucible Theatre in Sheffield. The theatre had sold out within a week before the show, and I must say she gave an incredible performance and an amazing demonstration of her mediumistic abilities. In the hotel after the show Doris and I were sitting having a glass of Champagne. She peered thoughtfully at me over her glass and said in a quiet voice, 'Your mother's going to pass soon.' I went cold and felt a little angry. My mother had only recently been taken ill and her condition not yet diagnosed. I looked at Doris in search of an explanation. 'She's been ill!' she continued, not even waiting for my response. 'She's got cancer, you know that don't you?' I shook my head, somewhat overwhelmed by her statement. As far as I was concerned my mother had been suffering from bronchial pneumonia and had developed some sort of respiratory complication, as a direct consequence. She wasn't in hospital but was due to go in for tests. As my mother was a fan of Doris Stokes, the following day she asked me if Doris had said anything about her to me. I didn't know what to say, and so I lied and said 'She had told me my mother Annie would be alright and that we must not worry.' I've often worried whether I did the right thing or whether I should have said nothing at all to my mother. Doris Stokes was, beyond a shadow of doubt, one of the twentieth century's best exponents of mediumship. Her warmth and caring maternal manner put everyone who received a message quickly at ease. I kept in touch with Doris right up until the day she died. In fact, she sent me a photograph of herself in her hospital bed surrounded by the Teddy Bears she had received from well-wishers. Sadly, she passed away during surgery to have a brain tumour removed, and today is still sadly missed by thousands of people who received help from her.

Although The Thought Workshop received donations from all over the world, because our overheads were so high, sadly we had to close. Almost at the same time as the centre's closure my mother was diagnosed with lung cancer, and in September of that year she died. Before she died she was in a coma for several hours. My brother, Alby, and his wife, Ethel and myself sat patiently around her bed, dreading what was to come. My mother began mumbling incoherently, and my sister-in-law said, 'Billy's here, Mam.' I never expected her to say what she did. 'Don't want him!' she murmured almost with hatred. 'Where's Albert?' Obviously referring to my brother. However, even he was a little surprised and somewhat embarrassed by what she had said. I was suddenly overwhelmed with a deep sense of sadness. I wanted to shake my dying mother and ask her 'what do you mean? Don't you love me? Please tell me you love me before you go'. But instead I made my excuses and slipped quietly to the bathroom. When I came back into my mother's bedroom, my sister-in-law said, 'She's gone, Billy'. She opened her eyes for a while, smiled, and as a single tear fell onto her cheek, she breathed her last breath and then closed her eyes for the very last time. I am not trying to say that my experience is unique, or that I am the only one who has lost a mother. I am only alive to day because of the way my mother nursed and looked after me as a child. I know she was in a coma, but I am sure that her feelings were there somewhere inside her head. Perhaps because of all the upset I had caused her over the years, her thoughts of anguish and pain were released at that moment. I have often wondered if my mother truly realised just how much power her last words had over my life. I want her to retract them but I know that she can't.

I have often heard mediums talking about seeing their mother's spirit leave the body as she died, but all that I saw was the woman who had brought me in to this world fading away before my eyes. At that moment nothing else mattered to me. I hated it and wanted that moment to go away. Sadly, though, that moment has haunted me ever since my mother died, and I suppose it always will.

WHO'S NELLY
Nelly Baxter was in her early seventies, a very good friend

and my confidante. I had known her several years, and because of kidney disease, had seen her health slowly deteriorate until she finally had to go on dialysis. Nelly sadly died in Sefton General Hospital before a kidney donor was found. Every time I drove passed Nelly's home I would always call in for a cup of tea and a chat, especially when I had a problem or was feeling down. My son Ben was only a few months old when Nelly died and so would not have remembered anything about her. Ben was now four years old, and I had been out with him for the day. I was driving passed Nelly's house and wishing that she was still alive so Ben and I could pop in for a chat, when suddenly my young son said, 'Daddy, who's Nelly?' I felt an icy chill pass over me and I pulled the car into the kerb. 'What do you mean?' I asked him gently. 'What made you ask that?'

'Who is Nelly, Daddy?' He asked again, an insistent tone to his voice.

'Nelly was a friend of mine.' I answered, urging him for an explanation. 'What made you ask that?'

Ben looked at me with his big innocent brown eyes, and putting his hands on his head, said, 'My head is speaking to me.'

'What do you mean, Ben?' I asked, now concerned by what he was telling me. 'What do you mean your head is speaking to you?' I could tell by the confused look on my son's face that this was the only way he could describe what he was experiencing. I decided not to push it any further, and knew that this was exactly how it all began for me when I was three years old. Ben obviously had mediumistic tendencies, and I just hoped that these would be kinder to him than they had been to me. I must admit, although I was a little concerned how it would affect my son emotionally, I was also comforted to know that Nelly Baxter was obviously still showing her motherly concern for me, and wanted to let me know that she was still around.

CHAPTER EIGHTEEN
TIMES THEY ARE A
CHANGING

In 1995 my career started to change quite dramatically, and it looked as though I was moving into new and very exciting areas, at least where my mediumship was concerned. Harper Collins published my autobiography, Beneath The Wings of Angels in March of that year, and I had also been asked to feature on a series of videos, to be called Billy Roberts Investigates the Paranormal. It now looked as though my long period of bad luck was coming to an end, and as the interest in mediums and the paranormal increased, I received more and more invitations to appear on various television and radio programmes. Multi-media contracted me to appear on the videos, on which I was to visit various haunted locations all across the northwest of England, long before the popular television programme, Most Haunted.

BILLY ROBERTS INVESTIGATES THE PARANORMAL
Although all three videos were fun to make, the one I enjoyed the most was the first in the series. The concept was the brainchild of Mel Donavon and Mike Tyrie of Multi-media productions, some years before the popular television programme Most Haunted was actually conceived.

Things went drastically wrong when we began filming the first video. We went to an isolated field somewhere on the Lancashire moors where they wanted me to do the introduction for the video. It was an extremely hot summer's day, and I was wearing a suit. For some reason best known to the producers, they needed me to stand precariously on a huge rock, primarily so they could film me from below. I have always been quite clumsy, and so the inevitable happened. I slipped back and landed in a mound of cow dung. It was awful and I stank to high heaven. I had to remain in my suit for the following two hours, and then I was given the opportunity to change in our host's farmhouse.

Our first venue was Chingle Hall in Goosnar near Preston, reputed to be the most haunted house in Britain. On this occasion I was accompanied by several other mediums whose job it was to use their psychic powers to 'home-in', so to speak, to any spirits that may be lurking there. Under my supervision a séance was held to see if we could encourage some paranormal activity or communication with discarnate souls. Apart from the mediums there were a couple of other guests, primarily invited by the producers to make up the numbers. The séance had been going for over half an hour without any interesting results. For a few moments I was out of camera shot and felt one of the producers tap me on the shoulder. 'This is awful!' He complained. 'Do something, Billy, or we'll have to pull out.' As I'd already put a lot of work into the project I certainly didn't want this to happen. Almost immediately I felt the presence of an elderly gentleman who hadn't long died. He spoke to me in a fairly weak voice and told me that his name was Rene. Although he did not sound French to me I knew that he was. As I knew most of the mediums present it was obvious that he belonged to one of the three invited guests. 'I have someone with me called Rene,' I said, feeling my heart pounding inside my chest. At first there was complete silence, and then a dark haired woman spoke up. 'Rene is my father,' she said, suddenly sobbing. 'He has not long died.'

I felt such a sense of relief that the connection had been made that I began to relax. This made the communicator clearer and much stronger. 'He wants you to know that he is with his mother now.'

The woman sobbed uncontrollably. 'Oh, yes,' she cried, nearly falling to her knees and being supported by the people either side of her. 'He loved his mother so much.' Although the producers had initially been quite sceptical about the whole project, they were extremely amazed and wanted more.

During the message Rene had given his daughter stern warnings about her health, telling her in no uncertain terms that she must stop smoking. As it turned out, the lady who received the message from her father was the wife of the owner of Chingle Hall. I have recently heard that some years later she passed away after being ill with cancer.

The second so-called haunted venue we visited was the George Public House on the High Street in Preston. This was an extremely small and very dismal pub with an oppressive atmosphere. The bar staff had reported shadowy figures when the pub was empty, and the beer pumps would operate by themselves even when not connected to a power source. Ashtrays would also slide unaided along the bar, and the toilet door would open and close by itself. It did have a spooky atmosphere and the cellar was even spookier. During some renovations and excavation of the cellar, workmen had unearthed a grave, obviously the remains of an old cemetery. Lying on top of the grave they found a gold wedding ring. Accompanied by fellow medium Agnes Davies we turned the old pub psychically inside out. Although I was aware of various discarnate figures, I was quite sure that they were not connected in any way to each other. One significant figure was a young man who had frequented the pub, and who had been knocked down by a wagon outside. An old man had been responsible for the opening and closing of the toilet door, and although he had been a regular drinking customer, he was just an integral part of the paranormal memory – a sort of a photographic image in the atmosphere and not a spirit at all.

Our final haunted location was very familiar to me – Woolton Hall in the suburbs of Liverpool. This is a fine old manner house built and designed by Robert Adam of fireplace fame. I had been putting on Seminars and Evenings of Clairvoyance there for 17 years, and so was only too familiar with its ghostly happenings. A friendly monk in green Wellington boots allegedly haunted the old Hall, once owned by the Catholic Church and a school run by nuns. It was believed that if the monk took a liking to someone he would allegedly follow them home seated in the back of their car. Although the atmosphere in Woolton Hall had always appeared quite warm and friendly to me, on this occasion I was there for a different reason and was able to 'home-in' to it in a completely different way. Whilst we were filming in one of the ornate upstairs rooms, a glass of water flew from the mantel across the room, smashing against the wall. Along with more than one expletive this was caught on camera as the producers Mel and Mike ran terrified from the room. There was no explanation for the phenomenon of the flying glass. I can only assume whoever or whatever was responsible did not approve of filming taking place. Personally, for me, this was the highlight of our visit to Woolton Hall even though many other things happened whilst we were there.

The second Video production we made was called GHOST FILES and was primarily a séance organised by television presenter and writer Kevin Horkin. During the séance an old friend and fellow medium, Diane Elliot from Manchester, joined me. Diane has an international reputation and is highly respected in the Spiritualist movement. Also taking part in the séance was Lynn Perrie (now deceased) of Coronation Street fame, Cynthia (Madam Sin) Payne, ex-society madam, Screaming Lord Sutch, ex-rock star and founder of the Raving Looney Party (now deceased); James Whale, television and radio presenter, Kevin Horkin and an anonymous guest. Although the producers had not said anything beforehand, the whole idea was for me to communicate with actress Pat Phoenix, (Elsie Tanner of Coronation Street,) a good friend of Lynn Perrie's. Apart from knowing what was common knowledge about the stars of Coronation Street, I knew virtually nothing else. As the pressure was on me to produce something, I must say I was extremely nervous. The anonymous guest was the first to receive a message from me. 'I've got a young woman with me,' I began, 'She has told me her name is Lyn. Do you understand this?'

The woman nodded and said 'Yes, I do.'

'I have a very strong feeling that she took her own life, is this true?' I added.

The woman became very emotional and just nodded her reply.

'Who is Peter?' I asked.

'Her husband.' She answered.

'Who is Pat?'

'That's me,' she replied, wiping the tears from her cheeks.

'She sends her love and says she is sorry.' I went on.

The woman was very distressed, and I paused for a moment.

'Will you accept that from me?' I concluded.

'Yes,' she nodded. 'Thank you, I will.'

At this point Diane took over and proceeded to give even more information to Pat, finishing the communication perfectly. She then began to give a message to Lynn Perrie from her mother. Lynn appeared somewhat confused. It was then that I realised that whilst everyone around the table had glasses of water, she had a glass of vodka. I could feel the producers' impatience and Mel was gesticulating from behind the camera. This distracted me so I called for the camera to stop filming so that they could say exactly what they wanted me to do. 'This is all too bloody slow and boring.' Complained the senior producer, Mike Tyrie. 'You're in charge of the séance Billy. DO SOMETHING.' Before another word was said a large red book was placed on the table in front of me. On the front of it was written THIS IS YOUR LIFE. It was the book that was presented to Pat Phoenix by Eamon Andrews on the long running television programme This is Your Life, and which was now owned by her friend Lynn Perrie. The producers wanted to make sure that Pat Phoenix made her presence felt. Pat Phoenix had died of cancer some years before, and Lynn Perrie had been given the famous red book as a memento of their friendship. Psychometry is not my forte but I knew I had to at least try. I Ran my fingers across the surface of the cover of the book and was immediately impressed by a poppy. There was a deadly silence across the table as everyone stared at me expectantly. I felt slightly uncomfortable but said the first things that came into my head. 'I can see the name Poppy.'

Lynn Perrie immediately responded. 'Poppies were Pat's favourite flowers. I took her some when she was in hospital.'

The Poppies seemed to bring Pat Phoenix close to me, and I could hear someone calling 'Jean'. It was a lady's voice, but I was sure it was not Pat Phoenix's voice. 'Who is Jean?' I asked.

'That's my real name.'

I went on to describe her mother and father who seemed to be expressing concern for someone called Steven. 'That's my son. He's not been too well.' Lynn Perrie answered, looking rather uncomfortable. 'He's got aids.'

'Your mum and dad are close to you.' I concluded that particular contact. And so the communication with the spirit world continued, with Lynn Perrie receiving a lot more evidence that her loved ones and friends were still giving her support from the other side of life.

The only person at the séance who did not receive a message was in fact David Sutch, more affectionately known as 'Screaming Lord Sutch.' Although he was a pleasant guy I did feel quite uncomfortable with him. I couldn't actually see anything at all with him. The more I tried to give him some sort of a message, the more difficult and clumsy it seemed. After suffering long bouts of depression, David Sutch in fact hanged himself some years later.

We finished filming Ghost Files around 4am. I was totally exhausted and had just started to get changed, when one of the producers called me to say that they had not filmed the introduction to the video. By this time I had no trousers on, and as my legs would be hidden under the table and out of camera shot, they went ahead and filmed me. People watching the video are completely unaware that during my introduction to the Ghost Files I am not wearing any trousers.

CHAPTER NINETEEN
GHOSTS OF A RADIO
STATION

I first met Pete Price, radio and television presenter, when he invited me on to his late night radio show to talk about my autobiography and to give readings on air. I must say we immediately hit it off and became friends. Although Pete always affirms that he is a sceptic, I have always argued this fact with him as I think that he himself is extremely psychic. Pete Price is an extremely professional performer, and I am quite sure that his scepticism is an important part of his public persona. One night when I was appearing on his programme, Pete told me that occasionally when he is in the studio by himself, late at night, the door opens by itself and things move on the console. Sometimes when he stands to retrieve some CDs from the rack, some invisible hand seems to move his chair away from the console. He said this freaks him out. At the time I thought that Pete was exaggerating things just for the sake of talking about something that would interest me. It wasn't until sometime later I was sitting in the studio listening to Pete talking on air to someone who had phoned in, when the studio door suddenly flung open wide causing Pete and myself to swing round. We both expected his producer or someone to walk in, but the door just creaked slowly closed again and an icy chill could be felt across the studio. We both shivered as we heard heavy footsteps across the carpeted floor. It didn't stop there. Later on Pete walked to the other side of the studio to return a C.D to the rack, and as he made his way back to his chair it rolled away from its position by the console, and did not stop until it had reached the other side of the room. We were both spooked, but Pete still affirmed his scepticism.

Another time I was appearing on Pete's show, he asked me to take part in a psychic experiment. I asked the listeners to hold broken watches or clocks, or should they be unwell to sit quietly and listen to my voice. I spoke for around 8 minutes, basically instructing them to relax and to focus their attention on whatever they were endeavouring to achieve. After this time we invited listeners to phone in and tell us what they experienced – if anything. We received stories of broken clocks and watches suddenly working, clocks stopping and even the hands on clocks moving backwards. In fact, lots of strange and weird things happened. As I was leaving the studio the phone lines went down, and Pete had problems playing music. More than this though strange ethereal sounding music could be heard over the music that was already being played. The studios engineers could not find the cause of the strange, disembodied music, and the phone lines remained down for over an hour, and then suddenly came back on without any prior warning. Since then Radio City along with Magic radio station have now moved to a different location and Pete's studio is presently at the top of what used to be the post office tower. I am waiting patiently for spooky things to happen there too.

CHAPTER TWENTY
THE BILLY ROBERTS
PARANORMAL STUDY
CENTRE

Some time around 1998 I decided to open a psychic study centre once again in Rodney Street. I am still not sure that this was the right thing to do. Nonetheless, it was something I felt I had to get out of my system. This was the third time I had been located in this famous road, and I always felt that each time I opened up there was going to be better than the time before. My mother always said that I lived in a dream world, even though my dad always argued that we are far more than our dreams. He also used to frequently say 'Never go back where you've already been!' When I was young this never made sense to me. However, today I know exactly what he meant. My first study centre was at 70 Rodney Street, and my second at 24. Now I had opened up at 55 Rodney Street. And the strange thing was Jimmy Iko, the bass player from the Kruzads, was now managing me. Jimi was a computer programmer, and I hadn't seen him since the band had disbanded in the sixties. In fact, all the members of the band had met up again by this time, thanks to Liverpool radio presenter, Pete Price. I was appearing on his late night show when Stevie Doyle, an old friend and keyboard player called in. After a little chat on air Pete suggested that the Kruzads reformed and play a spot on my approaching psychic stage shows. Without realising the consequences I agreed. I put myself in an awkward position, and had made an announcement on air. I had two big shows coming up over the next five months. One was at the Liverpool Empire, and the other at Southport Theatre. I then had the near impossible task of finding the lads from the Kruzads. Steve Barton as far as I knew was still living in France. Jimmy Iko and John Thompson were God knows anywhere. Paul Hitchmough, the Kruzads drummer, was living the life of a veritable recluse somewhere in Wales. Anyway, news travels fast on Merseyside, and although I was secretly hoping that nothing would come of it, within weeks all except John Thompson had got in touch. Talk about 'Wrinklies united,' is an understatement. All the lads, apart from Jimmy Iko, were recovering from something or other. Steve Barton, one of the original singers was also suffering from emphysema and was on more inhalers than me. Having got them all together I then had the arduous task of deciding exactly what we were going to do, and how the band would fit into my psychic stage show. What would the audience think? Heaven alone knew! After the initial shock to the Liverpool Empire and Southport Theatre's managers, we began rehearsing. Although it gradually became a self-indulgent exercise, I do have to admit I was in my element. Dixie Dean, a childhood friend of singer, Gerry Marsden, and also one of the original members of Gerry's original band, The Mars Bars, had formed the original Kruzads. Although Dixie had not been a part of this particular Kruzads, it seemed only right that he should be invited to join the line up for the two theatre shows. To play saxophone, flute and clarinet, my fifteen-year-old son, Ben was also invited to join us for the one-off appearances. It was a nightmare, and everything that could go wrong did go wrong, particularly the night before the first show, which was in Southport. Although I had told the lads to have an early night, they stayed out all night celebrating the band's reunion, and arrived at the theatre the following evening half-cut. I went ballistic! I had a responsibility to the audience and wanted it to be a good, and very professional show. How we got through it I'll never know - we did, and I vowed never again.

CHAPTER TWENTY ONE
TELEVISION APPEARANCES

With the publication of my autobiography, and the series of videos, I received invitations to appear on innumerable television programmes. It was late spring and I was recovering from a bout of flu, when I received a phone call from one of the producers of my videos. 'You're appearing on Big Breakfast', he informed me. 'You'd better be well enough for next Monday.'

As I'd never seen Big Breakfast I just mumbled with disinterest down the phone, and said I would be at his office in Swindon the following Sunday.

As Big Breakfast was broadcast quite early, we had to travel by car from Swindon in the early hours of the morning. I had no idea at all that the Big Breakfast was as zany as it was and that I would be treated with tongue in cheek and not taken seriously at all. At that time the presenters were Gabby Roslyn and Paul Ross. I must admit that both were very polite and I was treated a lot better than I thought I would be.

I thought I was there to be interviewed about my videos, and that is all, but Paul Ross announced that I was the psychic who was going to attempt to stop Big Ben the following week. I nearly died and glared angrily at my video producer, Mike Tyrie who was grinning from behind the camera. 'This morning though,' Paul Ross continued, 'Billy will endeavour to stop these clocks from working.' The camera panned around the studio where there were numerous miniature Big Bens strategically situated. I didn't know what I would do. Before I could say a word, Paul Ross turned to me. 'You've got 60 seconds Billy. Give it your best shot.' Thinking on my feet, I turned to the camera and began to speak to the viewers. I basically instructed them to mentally send their energies to the clocks in the studio, and to will them to stop working. I just hoped for the best as my time ran out. After checking all the clocks, Paul Ross announced. 'I'm sorry Billy; they are still ticking merrily away. What happened?'

I shrugged with embarrassment. 'Don't know Paul,' I said regretfully, shaking his hand in defeat. 'I have failed miserably.' Paul checked his wristwatch, and then looked at me with surprise. 'My watch has stopped!' He said, shaking his wrist. 'How did you do that?' He held his watch to the camera with disbelief. 'It's actually stopped!' Paul couldn't believe it, nor could I. His watch had stopped, and it looked to all intents and purposes that I had caused it to stop.

The problem was that far too many people took my experience on Big Breakfast far too seriously. I never really lived it down. Many of my fellow mediums criticised me for doing it in the first place, and others decried me for failing miserably. For me personally it was all just good fun and no more than that.

Big Breakfast was an experience – an experience I would not want to repeat. Strangely enough, of all the television programmes I have appeared on, more people actually recognised me on the street from Big Breakfast than any other. How unfortunate!

THE HORSE SPOILS THE SHOW

The Psychic Road show was a television programme that was to be hosted by celebrity astrologer, Russell Grant, and would feature different kinds of psychics and their skills. This was to be filmed at the Neptune Theatre in the Liverpool City centre, and I was told to be there at 9.30am prompt.

By the time the technicians had set everything up, and the camera crew were in place, it had gone 2pm and I was feeling somewhat jaded and did not feel like doing anything, let alone demonstrating clairvoyance.

One of the unusual psychic acts was a woman who claimed that she could talk to animals, primarily to find out what was troubling them. Her subject was a horse with emotional hang-ups. The producer of the show decided to leave this spot until later, and so accompanied by clairvoyant, Peter Richards, I was called to take my position at the back of the theatre. Russell Grant introduced us to a packed theatre, and together we quickly strode down the aisle towards the stage, from where we each gave three messages to selected members of the audience. After our demonstration, exhausted from the ordeal, we both withdrew to the green room to have a drink and dissect the ordeal. I must say I was glad when it was over and I was looking forward to seeing the following act – the psychic who could talk to animals. In this segment of the show the troubled horse was to be brought on stage and analysed by the psychic, who would then administer healing to alleviate its problem. As the Neptune Theatre was then above Halfords store, the only ways to the theatre were either up the stairs or in the lift, neither of which were feasible routes of access for a horse with psychological problems. 'No way!' I thought. 'Impossible!' As it happened, I was in fact proved right! The horse refused to go anywhere near the lift, and when it saw the stairs, became extremely agitated. As this topic was one of the main features of the television show, the whole programme was abandoned. What a waste of time, I thought. The horse did spoil the show and this was a whole day wasted. However, after seeing me demonstrate my mediumistic skills to a packed theatre, Russell Grant did invite me to appear on his Talk Radio programme, and he later appeared with me on one of my Psychic Stage Shows at the Beck Theatre in Hayes Middlesex.

SECRETS OF THE PARANORMAL

In 2002 I was asked to create and present my own paranormal series on Liverpool's Channel One Television, a cable channel that was televised throughout the Northwest. I accepted and within two weeks I recorded my first programme. I had previously formatted the series for a terrestrial channel that had not been broadcast, and so with all my guests already in place, I was ready to go. In the series I was to explore the whole spectrum of the paranormal, from Spiritual healing to the Aura, from haunted houses to mediums and clairvoyants. My son, Ben, composed and played the programme's theme music, and the first programme was an exploration of the aura. In this we put mediums to the test. After inviting two mediums, (who claimed to be able to 'see' the aura) to psychically analyse the auras of two anonymous volunteers, using a Kirlian colour camera, we then photographed their energy fields in an effort to either confirm or disprove what the psychics had said they had seen. The camera had confirmed exactly what both mediums, Terri Miller and Agnes Davies, had said, and the colours they had described were exactly what the aura camera had photographed. The first programme was a success and most certainly put mediums in a good light.

My second programme in the series was an investigative look at clairvoyants and mediums, primarily to determine whether or not they were all genuine. We selected three popular clairvoyants in the Northern seaside resort of Southport. I had lived there for ten years and knew that there were probably more clairvoyants in Southport than in any other town. The Clairvoyants featured in this programme were, Marie Woods, Bernice Robe Quinn and Jenny Pierce, and although all three came across as being extremely professional, Jenny Pearce's reading was uncannily accurate where I was concerned. In fact, Jenny gave me detailed information about what was going on in my life at that moment, and even highlighted events and projects that I was planning for the future. Although each clairvoyant had a very different style, in my opinion Jenny Pierce came across as the best and most effective exponent of mental mediumship, and the one who was more able to prove, beyond a shadow of doubt, that life was continuous. Ten out of ten for Jenny Pearce.

Although during the twenty-six week series I explored many different areas of both the paranormal and complimentary aspects of healing, for me personally, the most fascinating programmes had to be 'Haunted Houses' and 'Ghosts.' My main guest on the 'Ghosts' programme was local Liverpool writer of the Paranormal and historian, Tom Slemen. On Tom's suggestion we visited an office in Penny Lane, Liverpool (down the road from where my office is situated) where, it was alleged, a poltergeist occasionally caused havoc. Even though I had encountered poltergeist activity before, for some reason I must say that I was a little concerned about this one. I think that this concern was primarily due to the fact that it would be televised, and I did not want to find myself in an awkward position in front of the camera. When anyone is told that they are going to visit a so called 'haunted' location, the mind becomes involved and creates its own ghosts and demons, long before the haunted location is in fact reached. I am no exception, and by the time we reached the tiny office, just before the railway bridge in Penny Lane, my heart was pounding so hard against my chest, I thought I would pass out at any moment. Needless to say, I didn't let Tom know I was a little bit afraid, and I'm sure he didn't suspect anything. Unless of course, he was too polite to say anything. I am frequently asked if I am ever afraid, and I do have to admit that I do get frightened sometimes. Even though there are occasions when I have no choice but to deal with some spontaneous paranormal force, and usually know what exactly to do when confronted, I much prefer to be in control of the phenomena when they occur. I know it sounds quite silly but, it's the unexpected that unnerves me, and in this situation I had no idea what exactly to expect. All that Tom Slemen had told me was that there was a poltergeist present, and that the cause was believed to be a man who hanged himself sometime in the 1930s. More than this though I was not told. No sooner had we entered the little room at the back of the building than the cameras began to role. The pressure of having to produce something for the camera was almost as great as the fear I was feeling. I began to psychically home-in to the very oppressive and claustrophobic little room but could feel nothing at all! 'Sorry Tom,' I announced with some embarrassment, 'I don't feel anything!'

Because the cameras were still filming, I just kept talking and inwardly hoping that something would happen. No more than two minutes had passed when I became conscious of an old woman. I could see her quite clearly, standing in the corner of the room, staring at me. I could sense that she had been quite frail before she had died, and that she had taken her own life. I could sense nothing regarding the man who had allegedly hanged himself, and began to wonder whether this story was really true. In fact, I became psychically aware of quite a few discarnate personalities, none of whom had anything to do with the man who had hanged himself. In fact, the little room at the back of the building appeared to be some sort of epicentre for a variety of paranormal phenomena, which had collectively manifested as the poltergeist. Although nothing spectacular took place, the programme did make exceptionally good television.

A three story Victorian house in the Sefton Park area of Liverpool was the setting for my 'Ghosts' programme. The workmen refurbishing this magnificent old house had reported all kinds of strange happenings, from apparitions to objects moving around of their own accord. After completing their work for the day, brothers Craig and Mark Keatly, two of the workmen involved in the refurbishment, went from room to room checking that everything was secure for the night. As he was descending the stairs he noticed an elderly lady making her way up towards him. Thinking that it was a neighbour simply being curious about the extensive renovation, he invited her to take a look around. No sooner had he spoken to the woman than she smiled and then disappeared before his eyes. He couldn't believe what he was seeing and for a few moments was unable to move. Once he had collected his thoughts, he ran down the stairs and out of the house as fast as his legs would carry him, not stopping until he was standing by the door of his van.

Some weeks later both he and his brother were busying themselves in the wide hallway, when they noticed a young couple walking up the stairs. The couple were both about nineteen and were dressed in sixty's style clothes. The guy had long brown hair and was wearing a dark jacket and flared jeans, and the girl had shoulder length blond hair and was wearing a hippy style dress.

'Excuse me,' called Craig. 'Can I help you?' The brothers thought that the couple were planning to squat in the house and expected some trouble from them. They seemed to ignore Craig's question and he moved quickly to the foot of the stairs. 'Did you hear me?' he called angrily.' Where do you think you are going?' The couple still ignored him and continued to slowly ascend the stairs. When they reached the first landing, they turned to face the brothers and just disappeared without a word. Had mark not been there to witness the phenomenon with his own eyes he never would have believed it. After contacting me they agreed for us to film one of the programmes at the house.

I am usually very sceptical about these sorts of phenomena unless, that is, I can see it with my own eyes. We had been filming all day and, by the time we reached the house, it was after 6am and all the workmen had finished for the day. The brothers showed me round the house, reiterating what they had already told me as we went from room to room. Neither of the brothers appeared to me to be the kind of people who would make up something like this. They were both down to earth and extremely intelligent.

Whilst I was walking through one of the basement rooms, and trying to negotiate my way through bags of cement, tins of paint and other working utensils, I saw an old lady clairvoyantly standing in the doorway. She told me she had died in that room and that she had not been found for sometime. Not thinking that this information could be confirmed, I passed it on to one of the brothers. Craig grinned at me in disbelief. 'Amazing!' he retorted. 'Her body was so badly decomposed that it literally had to be scraped off the floor.' I felt an icy shiver pass through me and wanted to vacate the basement as quickly as possible. As I moved towards the door, a colleague held his digital camera in front of me.

'Look!' he said, somewhat ashen faced. 'Some sort of light anomaly!' He had seen a bright light to the right of me and photographed it. It was clearly a spirit light or, orb as the phenomenon is now known. However, this orb was not nebulous like the ones shown on the television programme Most Haunted, but was an intense sphere of white light, bright and clearly defined. We had captured something extremely significant on camera and were able to show this on television. For me personally this programme was by far the best of the series. In fact, Secrets of the Paranormal proved to be so popular I was contracted to do another ten-week series.

MALTESE TELEVISION

In 2002 I was invited to appear on a Maltese television

programme entitled Xarabank, a magazine programme hosted by an extremely sceptical and controversial guy by the name of Pepi Azzopardi. They put me up in a beautiful five star hotel right on the Mediterranean, and although I was only to work on the programme for two days, as a gesture of good will they paid for me to stay a whole week. This was quite an experience and the people of Malta were extremely friendly and very hospitable. My only concern was having to demonstrate clairvoyance before a studio audience composed of 200 staunch Catholics. On the Wednesday night I was to demonstrate my mediumistic skills to a capacity audience, and on the Friday night the recording of this would be reviewed by a priest, who was also the only exorcist on the island, and a psychologist. I had to be on top form, and my demonstration had to be good and very specific. I watched nervously as the studio filled up. The audience was predominantly female, with an age range from fifteen to eighty. Pepi had told me that as the programme would be edited, before beginning my demonstration I could talk to the audience, primarily to get the feeling of them. I did this for ten minutes before being given the signal to begin. My first contact was with a man in the Spirit World who told me his name was Lorenzo and that he had not long died. I spoke to a middle aged man in the front row. 'I have someone called Lorenzo here,' I said rather nervously, pausing for his response. For a moment I thought he wasn't going to answer me, but then he nodded.

'Lorenzo is my uncle,' he replied. 'He died two weeks ago.'

I breathed a sigh of relief and could feel a rush of excitement passing through the audience.

'He is with a young boy who appears to be looking for his daddy,' I continued.

The gentleman turned to a heavily set young man sitting beside him. 'This is my son,' he informed me, gesturing for him to speak.

'You have my son,' the young man replied emotionally. 'He was five when he died.' I felt somewhat excited and very relieved.

'Lorenzo is saying that you have his ring and watch,' I continued, 'and that they are both engraved.' I went on.

'That is correct!' replied the man's son, holding up his hand to show that he was wearing both items of jewellery.

My contact then quickly changed and I found myself listening to another man speaking to me from the Spirit World.

'I am looking for Maria,' I said hesitantly. 'It sounds like Maria Bussattil.'

A lady politely put up her hand in response.

'That is my name.' She said in a quiet voice. She looked as nervous as I had initially felt.

'I have your husband with me,' I said. 'He tells me his name is Frederick.'

The dark haired lady broke down and was immediately comforted by her daughter who was also crying.

'He is telling me he was so poorly,' I paused for a moment. 'You bathed his feet in water.'

Both the woman and her daughter cried. 'We took him to the beach,' sobbed his daughter, 'and I bathed his feet in salt water.'

I continued to pass on other personal information before moving to someone else.

The demonstration went well and after an hour I took a short break. During the break Pepi told me that, to enable them to obtain enough footage, I would have to continue demonstrating for at least five hours. I couldn't believe what I was hearing. 'No way!' I blurted. 'I couldn't possibly work that long!'

Pepi just shrugged his shoulders and walked away. Before I started working again, the agent who had booked me to do the show came over to talk to me.

'Billy,' she said quietly, 'I am so sorry, but you will have to carry on as Pepe has said. If you do not they will refuse to pay your fee and your hotel bill.'

I felt so annoyed and completely let down. When I had initially been booked to do the programme they had certainly not made it clear exactly what they wanted me to do. Perhaps it was my fault because I had been too eager to visit Malta. I was already extremely tired and felt so hot under the studio lights that my clothes were sticking to my body. However, I somehow managed to get through the evening, only to be told at the end of the demonstration that I had to do three private consultations. I did these and couldn't wait to return to my hotel and fall into bed.

To everyone's great surprise, on the Friday night the entire audience from the Wednesday demonstration returned to support me. A recording of my performance was shown to everyone. The priest said that it was impossible to talk with the 'dead' and that only Jesus was able to do that. Pepi asked him 'But Father how does Billy Roberts do that?'

'I don't know!' he replied, 'But he is working with the devil.'

The audience protested loudly and shouted their support.

'But Billy gave me my uncle's name – Lorenzo,' said the middle aged gentleman. 'What have you to say about that?'

The psychologist interjected his opinion. 'Lorenzo is a common name in Malta!' he retorted smugly. 'He most probably guessed it.'

Both the priest and the psychologist had an answer for everything, and it was clear to me that where they were concerned I was fighting a losing battle. However, the audience was totally with me, and those who had received messages from me on the Wednesday showed their support all evening.

My trip to Malta was most certainly one I shall never forget.

CHAPTER TWENTY-TWO
POLTERGEISTS AND
THINGS THAT GO
BUMP IN THE NIGHT

Nobody could ever accuse me of having a boring career, for nothing could be further from the truth! As well as working as a medium, I suppose you could also define me as a paranormal investigator or, 'Ghost hunter', for the want of a better name. Over the years I have been invited to look at all manner of so-called haunted locations, many of which have been a complete waste of time. Whenever a person is pre-warned before being invited to a hunted house, usually his or her mind creates its own ghosts and demons, long before they actually reach the location. This is the very nature of expectation and fear. With this in mind, whenever I am invited to a place where paranormal disturbance has occurred, I do my very best to disregard what I have been told to expect when I get there. This way I have an unbiased approach, necessary when making a detailed analysis about paranormal phenomena.

Although I am interested in all areas of the paranormal, I am particularly fascinated by the haunted house phenomenon, especially poltergeist activity and the different ways in which poltergeists manifest. Some years ago I received a phone call from a businessman in Southport. He sounded quite nervous, and I expected him to hang up at any moment. He explained that he owned property in and around the Southport area, and that he was having difficulty selling one particular Victorian house. 'There's something strange going on!' he stuttered. 'I don't believe in anything like this, but my daughter suggested that I contact you to see if you can help.'

It was quite obvious that he was a sceptic and had contacted me as a very last resort.

The man told me that it was a large, three-story detached house, set in acres of land, and situated in the same road as the famous Palace hotel. Now I was interested. Although no longer there, the Palace Hotel was built in 1866 and was a landmark in the popular seaside resort of Southport. When it had been completed, to the architect's sheer horror, it had been erected facing the wrong way. Instead of looking out to the sea, this magnificent building faced inland. This caused the architect, William Magnall to fall into a depression. He committed suicide by jumping off the roof of the hotel. His death seemed to precipitate all sorts of paranormal phenomena, such as the lifts operating by themselves, even after the power source had been disconnected. Disembodied hands seemed to turn lights on and off, and eerie sounds were frequently heard echoing down the deserted corridors. Its popularity eventually waned, and for a long time the hotel stood empty, a ghost of what it once was. It was eventually demolished, and all that remains of the hotel is the old coach house, which is now The Fishermens Rest Public House.

The house I was called to was situated in the same road. Although I was quite excited about visiting the haunted house, I was also quite nervous. The man had apparently invited various mediums to see if they could sort the problem, but each one had fallen violently sick, and had made a hasty retreat.

When I entered the old house, it was clear that it had been quite magnificent in its day. The hallway and downstairs rooms were a shambles, and looked like a derelict house during the blitz. Although the man was keen for me to investigate the downstairs rooms where, he informed me the furniture was constantly thrown about by unseen hands, I felt inclined to follow my curiosity up the broad staircase. A stained-glass window filtered the sunlight, casting an array of colours onto the top landing. It was mesmerising, and I stood halfway up the stairs for a few moments, watching the colours play across my path. I was suddenly overwhelmed by a pungent smell, rather like burning rags, and without any warning, a blue vase flew from its resting place on a table at the top of the stairs, and then landed gently on the floor a few feet in front of me. I followed my gaze to the landing under the stain-glass window, and then was immediately picked up at least two inches by some unseen force, and was then thrown with my face to the wall. I was suspended above the ground for a few seconds, possibly longer, and then I felt an excruciating pain in my stomach. This lasted for five or so minutes. I knew that I had to remain in the house and not leave as the other mediums had done, as this would only give whatever was causing the paranormal disturbance more power. After sometime exploring the upstairs rooms, the spirit of an elderly man made contact with me. He told me that he had hanged himself after suffering with a long illness, sometime in the mid nineteenth century. Even though the old man would not leave me alone, I knew he was not the perpetrator of the poltergeist activity, and that some other malevolent force was responsible. I never like to admit defeat, but in this case I really had to. There seemed to be more than one disruptive force, and I really did dread to think what they were! After spending two hours making a detailed analysis of the old house, I concluded that nothing would ever be done to eliminate the 'odd goings on' completely. I told the man that a foreign businessman would eventually buy the house from him, and that it would be demolished and a new house built in its place. Some years later I learned that that's exactly what happened. A rest home for the elderly now stands where the old house stood. Although it is possible to demolish the bricks and mortar, and get rid of the physical structure completely, the subtle nature will remain. So too will its ghostly inhabitants. This means that any paranormal activity previously experienced before the house was demolished, will most certainly still persist. I often wonder whether the elderly residents of the rest home are bothered by the same phenomena, or whether they are completely oblivious to the ghostly goings on as they go about their daily lives. I wonder!

Although somewhat of a cliché, 'Seeing is believing' has always been my policy. People tend to exaggerate the things they experience, and so regardless of what I am told goes on in a so-called haunted location, I really do have to see it for myself. On another occasion a distraught middle-aged lady whose son had been killed in a car accident some years before contacted me. She explained that her son used to call to have something to eat with her ever evening at 6pm prompt. Two months after his death she would see him sitting in his usual place, a look of complete distress across his ashen face. 'He comes every night at the same time!' she went on. 'And he is as solid and tangible as he was when he was alive!'

Had it not been for the woman's obvious anguish I would have made my excuses and given her another medium's phone number.

I called to her home in a very quiet and middle class area of Liverpool, just before 6pm the following night. The well-spoken lady insisted that I should not sit in his chair, and that I should sit with her on the settee under the window. Although I wasn't really expecting anything to happen, I was still quite excited just with the possibility alone. However, to my surprise, and just as the woman had said, at 6pm prompt a grey swirling mist seemed to collect on the young man's chair. Within seconds it began to take the shape of a person sitting there. It remained quite indistinct for at least five minutes, before metamorphosing into the clear figure of a young man with shoulder-length hair. As the woman had said he looked ashen faced and quite distressed. Although he did not make any contact with me, the woman appeared to have some telepathic connection with him, and this seemed to delight her. I couldn't fathom the whole thing, until I recalled that the woman had told me her son had a small terrier called Jip, and that they were inseparable. His dog had also been killed in the accident, and yet it was not with him. It suddenly dawned on me that this just might be the problem. I explained to the woman that her son might be distressed because he couldn't find his dog. At first she didn't seem to understand what I meant, until I went on to explain that the accident may have caused their separation, and that if her son and his canine companion were reunited, he would then be more settled and leave her alone.

She kept asking her son if Jip was with him. I told her to keep asking the question over and over. She did, and all of a sudden, seemingly from nowhere, the little dog appeared. The playful little terrier sat at the young man's feet, looking lovingly up at him, obviously in an effort to be noticed. Nothing else was said, and both the young man and his dog just disappeared into nothingness without warning.

That was probably one of the most unusual and very touching experiences I have ever had, and a case of 'seeing is truly believing.'

Of course, not all paranormal investigations are as interesting, and many are simply a waste of time. However, the one thing I have learnt over the years is never to be too complacent when receiving a request for help. Although the majority of investigations prove to be a complete waste of time, there is a minority that turn out to be astoundingly interesting.

CHAPTER TWENTY-THREE
NEW ORLEANS AND
GHOST HUNTER

In 2003 I received a phone call from a young lady called Perelandra Blanche from Sony Computer Entertainment. 'We wondered if you'd be interested in taking part in a documentary to promote our new Playstation 2 Game, Ghost Hunter?' She asked. 'Although there wouldn't be a large fee, the project would have its rewards.'

The Kudos just doing something for Sony alone was indeed payment in itself, and so I invited her to my office in Penny Lane.

The chatty young woman arrived with a camera crew, 'just to take a few shots,' she explained, 'to see how you look on camera.'

In fact, Perelandra Blanche made me an offer I simply could not refuse. She went on to explain that the documentary was to be filmed in New Orleans, the epicentre of blues and jazz, and a place I had always wanted to visit. I said 'yes' immediately. 'When do we leave?'

Perelandra spent nearly two hours explaining the concept of the documentary, which was extremely 'spooky' in itself. Two guys had developed the Ghost Hunter Game, completely unaware that the haunted locations they had created in their game actually existed in New Orleans.

The game portrayed a retired policeman who went in search of malevolent spirits, with the sole intention of destroying them. A haunted Second World War Battleship that had been sunk with hundreds of fatalities was the first venue on the game. They had discovered that the real ship was in a dry dock museum on the Gulf of Mexico.

131

Accompanied by New Orleans parapsychologist, Kalila Smith, I spent three hours wondering around this World War Two vessel, looking for any signs of paranormal activity. Although I am claustrophobic, accompanied by the camera crew, I had to go into the engine room, in the very bowels of the ship. Disembodied voices seemed to echo all about us, and ghostly shadowy figures were also caught on camera. Both Kalila and I saw the ghostly figure of an officer waving his fist in anger from where he was standing on the bridge. The ship had been sunk by the Japanese in 1944, and was raised from its watery grave once the war had ended. The proud war-torn ship was so alive with paranormal activity that even the cameras kept malfunctioning.

Our second haunted venue was a plantation house, two miles down the road from the house featured in the classic film, Gone With The Wind. This was the plantation house that is seen on the label of the well-known liqueur, Southern Comfort, and was the plantation where slaves were allegedly raped and murdered. This was obviously the epicentre for an incredible amount of paranormal activity, most of which was visually apparent. The camera lens zoomed in and out even when they were not connected to any power source, and strange lights appeared to move upon and down the disconnected cables. The most spectacular thing for me was the spirit of a young, and very mischievous girl playing by the rocking chair on the porch. No sooner had I told the camera crew what I could see when the chair began to rock backward and forward, seemingly to all intents and purposes, by itself. A young black female slave servant had apparently poisoned the lady of the house and her two children, and because the other slaves were punished for her misdemeanour, they beat her to death. Although now long since gone, the sadness emanating from the energies it had created, could most certainly be felt, and the spirits of those who had died there were still very much in evidence.

Our final investigation was a haunted graveyard deep within the Louisiana swamps. We travelled down the Mississippi in a small tourist's boat, chugging our way through the green moss-covered water towards our destination some miles away. With the sun low on the horizon, like a huge ball of fire slowly sinking into the Mississippi, we pushed our way relentlessly through the murky water, with a thousand curious alligator eyes watching and waiting. The journey down the Mississippi River was quite frightening in itself, let alone what I had to do once we reached our destination. At that point all I had been told was we were going to a graveyard, but more than that they would not say. I remarked to one of the guides that I could not swim should the boat sink. I did not like his response. 'I wouldn't worry about that!' he joked. 'The gators will get you anyway.'

It seemed to be an age before the monotonous sound of the chugging engine final stopped, and the boat slowly coasted into the reedy bank of the river. By now the sun was setting fast, and the sky was ablaze with a veritable kaleidoscope of colours that filtered through the trees before dividing into innumerable dancing shadows. Not too far away I could distinguish the silhouettes of several crosses, strategically marking out the graves in the cemetery, and as soon as the boat pulled into its final resting place, an owl hooted, and some other unknown creature howled. Although an ideal setting for a spooky documentary, I secretly wished that the whole eerie scenario was being filmed in a studio somewhere, and that I was not waiting to enter a haunted graveyard deep within the Louisiana swamps.

As the last of the sunlight filtered through the trees, a crescent moon had already appeared, casting even more eerie shadows over the whole overgrown terrain.

'Julia Brown was a Voodoo Queen!' explained Kalila Smith, the parapsychologist. 'She was taunted by German settlers who lived in a village in the swamps. They made her life a misery, and so she got her revenge by placing a curse upon them. A hurricane struck the village and killed everyone except a 12-year-old girl and an elderly black man. Not content with exacting revenge upon the village, she then cursed the young girl and the old man. The old man was killed in a freak accident, and although the girl grew up and had a family of her own, they all died of a mysterious illness.' The producer then went on to explain that the German Villagers had been laid to rest in the graveyard, but their spirits still roamed the swamps in search of Julia Brown.

It all sounded amazing, but I wasn't sure exactly what they wanted me to do.

Accompanied by the camera crew, Kalila and I wended our way between the crooked wooden crosses, and whilst I related to the camera what I was feeling, she scrutinised the reading on the dial of her EMF meter. I saw something moving in my peripheral sight, and swung my head round to see several diminutive figures of light running across the open area ahead. Kalila explained that soldiers had pursued a small tribe of pygmy natives who had been living in the swamps. Once they were caught, they were decapitated and their heads impaled on wooden stakes strategically placed throughout the swamps. The sight of these mischievous creatures sent an icy chill through me, and I wanted to abandon the whole project. I couldn't, of course, and remained where I was almost in the centre of the graveyard.

When the fading sunlight had disappeared completely, the moon continued to cast its pale light over the swampland. We continued to make our way deeper into the graveyard, and when I turned to speak into the camera, everyone gasped in unison. They had obviously seen something I had not. Because of the continuous cacophony of swamp sounds I had not heard the white owl that had spread its wings above my head, before flying off somewhere into the trees. According to ancient American Native folklore this phenomenon portends death, particularly when you hear the owl call your name.

After this unnerving experience we witnessed light anomalies moving quickly across the wooded area ahead of us, and disembodied voices whispering in the still night.

The strange thing was, I was the only person there who was not bitten by mosquitoes. Maybe they did not like my blood.

I was so glad when the camera crew packed their equipment and we had boarded the small boat to make our way back down the Mississippi River to New Orleans. Although very frightening, my trip into the Louisiana swamps was one I would not have missed for the world. Spooky, but extremely fascinating!

CHAPTER TWENTY-FOUR
MORE CHANGES

Sadly, when he was 19 my son, Ben, and I had a disagreement. As my car stopped at the traffic lights, after an angry outburst, Ben jumped out and ran off down the road. That was four years ago and I haven't seen him from that day to this. Although my son is a multi-talented musician, and had been offered places in Manchester College of Music and the world renowned LIPA, founded by Paul McCartney, he chose to give it all up to work for a major insurance company. As far as I know Ben is living in Glasgow, and my birthdays and Father's days come and go without even a card. Although Ben is my son and I love him very much, he is the biggest disappointment in my life. He has broken my heart and I do hope one day he will realise that. I know it is a cliché and something that my mother and father used to say to me, but he will regret it all when I have gone - then, it will be too late!

Although at the moment my French son is living in Worthing, at the other end of the country, he and his wife, Tina, are considering coming back to the north of England to live. At least then we can see them more often.

In 2006 I married Dolly, my partner of six years, and because I had been married before, even though she hadn't, we could not marry in church, which was something she desperately wanted more than anything in the world. It was suggested that we should approach a United Reformed Church whose policies are not as strict as other churches. In fact, The United Reformed Church had nothing whatsoever against marrying divorced people, and were only too willing to offer us a choice of dates. And so, on September 2nd 2006 we got married in Christ Church in Port Sunlight, and Dolly had exactly the wedding she wanted. Sadly, though, her mother had passed away a few years before, and a family disagreement prevented her three sisters from being there on the day. We secured the whole of the Hillbark Hotel in Frankby, and so all our guests had rooms in the picturesque country hotel, set in acres of parkland. Our friend, Eithne Browne, the television actress was one of the guests, and she even did the speech at the church. Kiki Dee, the singer was also a guest and she did a half-hour spot with Carmello her excellent guitarist, making the whole day absolutely perfect. I had first met Kiki in 1995 when she came to one of my seminars in Luton, but I had always been a huge fan, and to actually have her sing at our wedding was the proverbial icing on the cake. Because Dolly had no family to give her away at the wedding ceremony, our good friend, Mary Johnson, the Lord Mayor of Wirral's wife, gave her away. Another guest at our wedding was our good friend, Dr Ciaran O'Keeffe, parapsychologist on the popular television programme, Most Haunted. In fact, Ciaran and I have written a book, entitled *The Great Paranormal Clash*, published by Apex Publishing Ltd, in which we take an in-depth look at mediumship and the paranormal.

Our wedding day could not have been any better, and all the guests were collected from their homes in a stretch limousine. We had eight fabulous stretch limos and two Rolls Royce. Dolly was collected in a pink Rolls and I was collected in a blue one. My French Son, Benjamin and my nephew, Alby, shared the responsibility of best man, and both gave speeches.

The day was filmed by a camera crew from London, who were to use part of what was filmed about my life, for a programme to be broadcast on Channel Four television. Sadly, along with cameras and other filming equipment, the footage was destroyed in a fire at the producer's home in

France. Luckily no one was injured in the fire, but without the video footage, the only record we had of our wedding day were the photographs. The wedding was very nearly called off because money Dolly was expecting wasn't transferred into her account when it should have been. However, the money came two days before, and that's exactly when we got the wedding rings, and Dolly bought her wedding dress the day before the actual wedding, on September 2nd 2006. In fact, she was lucky enough to get a dress that fitted her straight off the peg. Everything fell into place at the last minute, and no one at the wedding knew anything about it. Little wonder we both looked extremely stressed and very tired.

CHAPTER TWENTY-FIVE
AND FINALLY, MY FAMILY
AND THE HELL I CREATED

All through my life I have had to struggle in one way or another. My health has always prevented me from leading a completely normal life, and even as a child allowances were frequently made because of the fact that I suffered with Bronchiectasis. This debilitating condition meant that my lungs constantly filled with sticky, often foul smelling mucus, and so they had to be emptied three to four times a day. This was achieved through postural drainage, a tiring and very time consuming process that necessitated my back being pounded whilst I was lying in a horizontal position. I still have to do this three or four times a day in order to keep my lungs empty and free of infection. Apart from my health problems though, from a very early age I was always made to feel different, and definitely not like other children. I am quite sure now that this did a lot of damage to me psychologically speaking and contributed to my drug dependence and ultimate addiction in later life. Although all that is now history, today I still have a constant struggle on my hands.

I think the most difficult thing for a medium to have to face is the criticism from family and old friends. 'Where did that come from?' is a typical question. 'You weren't a medium when I knew you as a child.' is another. In fact, mediums have an awful lot to contend with and are frequently forced to face a barrage of questions, very often designed to embarrass and ridicule. Unless the medium's family have been privy to his or her experiences they are very often unaware that their family member is a medium. Even though I have been working as a professional medium for over 25 years I still have to contend with sarcastic remarks and carefully veiled innuendoes from my family. 'Don't remember you being psychic,' is my niece's favourite comment. 'Why aren't I psychic and you are?' Is another of her comments, always made in the presence of other people. Although my brother never really offers an opinion one way or another, I know he thinks it. The truth is, my brother left home when I was around 9 years old and we never saw him for five to six years. A high percentage of my experiences took place during his absence, and my niece was not even born then. I used to resent the sarcasm and little jibes, but today I am much older and wiser. Today when a remark is made by anyone who thinks they know me, I simply retort, 'you can fool some of the people some of the time, but you most certainly can't fool all of the people all of the time.' I have been working as a medium for far too long and have built up a respectable reputation. It is sad that I can never talk to my family about my work and all the exciting things I have done, but I just can't. They are just not interested and really do believe that what I do is all trickery, at least where I am concerned anyway. My nephew is the only one in my family who has seen me demonstrate my mediumistic skills in a theatre, and I still do not know how he feels about it. Although I love my brother and his family very much, my profession as a medium is more important to me than anything, and I would therefore not allow anyone to jeopardise it. It's not only my family that have been problematic for me - old friends and neighbours too have made their snide and sarcastic comments. One old neighbour even telephoned a radio programme I used to appear on regularly. 'I remember Billy Roberts with long hair and being so incoherent he couldn't even talk,' was the comment made to broadcaster Pete Price on his popular Magic Radio programme. This comment was obviously tailored for maximum hurt and to embarrass and ridicule me. Fortunately, though, Pete told the caller in no uncertain terms, 'that was then but people change and some develop spiritually. Besides, Billy Roberts has hidden nothing – read his autobiography.' The guy in question had obviously not read my autobiography and was put quickly in his place. I am quite sure that all mediums go through the same thing at some time in their lives. Unfortunately, because of my past I have a lot more than most to contend with.

Unfortunately, Pete Price does not speak to me anymore. And so, to put the record straight with him, and to clear any misunderstandings, I decided to write this. When I returned from my visit to New Orleans, Pete Price phoned me to ask if I would appear on his late night radio programme. I told him that I had not been too well, and that I had been coughing blood, (a symptom of Bronchiectasis) and after expressing his concern he said I could appear the following week. As soon as I put the phone down, the producer of Billy Butler's programme, a well known Radio Merseyside presenter and an opposing station, phoned me to see if I would come to the radio station for a ten minute interview in the afternoon. As Pete's programme was on air until quite late, I didn't think anything about it and accepted the offer. That evening Pete announced that due to illness I would not be on his show. The switchboard went berserk, with Pete's listeners eager to snitch on me by telling him I had been on Billy Butler's programme in the afternoon. Needless to say Pete Price did not understand, and although I had known him for a long time, Pricey, (as he is affectionately known,) just did not want to know. I did try to contact him with the offer of working with me on some theatre shows, but he declined, saying 'thanks, but no thanks.' However, I still have the greatest of respect for Pete Price, and still think he is an extremely talented entertainer, even though he is stubborn, amongst other things.

My work as a medium has never been dull or boring, and every day presents something completely different. I have travelled all over the world and appeared on television and stages in many different countries; I've been subjected to all sorts of psychic attacks and frequently found myself being scrutinised and tested by psychologists, parapsychologists and psychiatrists in universities and in clinics of one kind or another. Only those who are close to me know exactly what I go through on a daily basis, where I have been and what I have achieved. When my mother, Annie died I lost my greatest and dearest friend. She was the only one who understood me and knew exactly what was going on in my mind. To be perfectly honest I am only alive today because of my mother and how exactly she looked after me when I was a child. When she died my Aunty Sadie (my mother's half sister) took over. She too helped me immensely right up until the day she died in 1998.

Since approaching this book's conclusion, my work has changed yet again. The Trinity Mirror Group have published my first children's book, The Magic Locker, a fantasy book inspired primarily by my long stays in Alder Hey Hospital as a child. Although children's hospitals are today completely different to when I was a child in the 1950s, for the majority of children staying in hospital is very often a frightening experience. In hospital as a child I would imagine that a diminutive cartoon-like figure would visit me via the locker beside my bed. Accompanied by the little man, known to me as The Sleepy Time Keeper, my imagination would transport me through the locker door and into a magical world of fantasy, peopled by crazy and very surreal characters. This book was illustrated and published in July 2008. Part of the proceeds will be donated to the IMAGINE appeal at Alder Hey Children's Hospital. I have now also written the script and music for the musical stage version, which will be launched for one week at The Liverpool Empire, beginning in September 2009. Although my work has changed somewhat, I still feel that it is still spiritually inspired.

CHAPTER TWENTY-SIX
SHADOWS OF THE FUTURE

I first became acquainted with The Elders sometime in 1990. As far as I understood they were a group of mystical discarnate beings, represented by Tall Pine. TP explained that although I had only just become aware of them, they had always been involved in my life in one way or another. My work with the Elders really began to evolve some time around the autumn of 1990 when I became aware of them during a period of intense meditation. Through Tall Pine they started giving me their insights into future situations and events, and particularly highlighted world issues, climatic changes, significant catastrophes, wars and the deaths of leading figures. When all this began to happen I felt reluctant to take notice. It made me quite depressed and I was always left with a morbid feeling after meditation. At this time I did have a very close relationship with Tall Pine and I was able to express my concern and displeasure about the prophetic observations they were giving me. T.P made me understand that it was not their intention to depress me but to allow me to access incredible data about the future history of the planet and mankind. Initially I had great reservations and was apprehensive about meditating. The majority of prophecies that were given were in fact about doom and gloom events, and were very rarely uplifting or joyful. 'This is the nature of your mind,' commented Tall Pine. 'It is primarily a case of perception – that is how you yourself perceive and interpret what we give you.'

I decided to comply with their wishes and go along with their plan. They called the prophecies 'SHADOWS OF THE FUTURE,' and were a fairly comprehensive collection of interesting and significant insights into the future. At one point I abandoned the project thinking that it was all in my mind. Tall Pine made it clear to me, saying, 'you are correct! It is all in your mind. The problem is do you trust your mind? Do you trust the things you know? And more importantly, how will you compare the things you now know with the things you will one day know, but presently do not? The things you now know were once things you did not know. The concept is quite simple as long as you trust your own mind.'

The one thing I had always learnt about Tall Pine is that he has an extremely good sense of human, and tends to speak in parables and clichés – but he's never wrong. I have learnt that much about him.

DIANA PRINCESS OF WALES

When I had completed the book of prophecies I was commissioned by the Woman's Realm magazine to make some predictions for the Millennium. I carefully selected some from my book and included the very shocking and yet controversial prediction about the death of Diana Princess of Wales that I had been given some years before. Although I received payment from the magazine, primarily because of the Diana prediction they refused to publish.

When the Shadows of the Future was first compiled, primarily because of the subject matter, I was very reluctant to send the book to a publisher, but then some of the prophecies began to actually happen. Mount Etna, which had been dormant for 100 years suddenly, began to erupt. The Elders also foretold of friction in certain countries and, in particular, the beginning of the war in Iraq. It was all beginning to take place. The only criticism was that the time scale was out. The Elder's excuse was that time in their world has a completely different meaning, which is why the time of some of the prophecies were slightly out. Then, during one of my regular appearances on the James Whale Talk Radio Show in London, the controversial presenter put me on a spot by asking me to reveal some of the prophecies. The most controversial one in the book was about the death of Princess Diana. The Elders had revealed that she would meet her untimely death in an automobile accident in France, accompanied by a wealthy foreign entrepreneur. The Talk Radio switchboard went crazy that night with listeners wanting to express their protestations about what I had said. I must admit I did feel like hiding away for a while and was extremely embarrassed about the 'on-air' prophecy. I didn't want it to come true but had a strong feeling that it would. When Diana was killed I was driving back from a seminar in London. It was about three in the morning when I heard the announcement on the radio that Dodi had in fact been pronounced dead, and that Diana's condition was unknown. Before I had reached my home in Southport the second announcement was made that Diana the Princess of Wales had died at the scene of the accident. I was so shocked that I had to pull into the side of the road. I felt as though I couldn't breathe and felt an overwhelming sense of loss, as though a personal friend had died. The following morning my phone did not stop ringing. First of all James Whale's producer contacted me to make an appearance on his programme to discuss the prediction, then the ex-editor of The Woman's Realm contacted me. She had found my original predictions quite interesting and had decided to keep them. She asked my permission to try and sell them to another magazine. Of course, because of the delicate nature of the prediction itself nobody wanted to know. Most magazines found it distasteful and a little obscene. Eventually the story was sold to EVA Magazine for £500, which we donated to Alder Hey Children's Hospital. After Shadows of the Future and the Diana prophecy I decided not to allow the Elders to channel any more through me – at least for a while.

However, more recently they have begun to channel Shadows of the Future – Secrets of the Past, containing more startling revelations about the future of mankind. However, these prophecies are even bleaker and very depressing!

CHAPTER TWENTY-SEVEN
I BELIEVE IN ANGELS

Although sceptics and the media frequently ridicule the very notion of Spirit Guides, there is nonetheless a growing interest today in Spirit Guides and Angelic forces. It's only human nature to hope that some invisible force is watching over us, and guiding us through the turmoil of our lives. In fact, the one thing that has sustained me during my very difficult life is my belief in angels and the intervention of Divine forces. I am not talking about the traditional archetypal angel with wings as depicted in the bible, but more the pure angelic beings whose sole desire is to help those less fortunate. I have always been aware of angelic forces guiding me and have always known that they were there observing me from the periphery of my life. As a small child I was extremely aware of angels, gentle beings cloaked in white gowns of light who always brought to me feelings of peace and solace. Although today I no longer see angels in that way, I have come to the logical conclusion that children 'see' things as they really are, and that their perception of this world and beyond is untainted. We adults often become arrogant and complacent, and it is these negative qualities that lower the veil that separates our world from the world of angels.

Although Angelic beings are somewhat different from the spirit guides associated with Spiritualism and mediums, Angels are the Supreme Hierarchy and spirit guides their ambassadors. Angels have mostly lived out their existences in the supersensual side of the universe without ever having had an experience of a physical existence. Although they possess great powers, such powers are primarily used to influence one's judgement rather than to initiate miraculous changes in one's life. This is not to say that they do not cause miracles to happen – they can and frequently do. However, without the appropriate internal transformation any angelic intervention would be transitory and impermanent. I have always felt that a belief in angels is a prerequisite for my work as a medium, and without that belief there would be absolutely no point to it. Occasionally there are glimpses of an angel in the eyes of certain individuals whose spirituality, kindness and compassion makes them stand out from everyone else. We frequently see an angelic force manifesting in some animals, such as in our pet cat or dog, which may seem different from other animals. I have no doubt that angels frequently make their presence felt in many different ways. Prayer precipitates angelic forces and prayer is more often than not the 'key' that unlocks the 'Great Door' that they might access our lives.

One of the greatest Spiritualist misconceptions is that angels will always guide us along the easiest road – this is not so. I have learnt that very little is achieved in a life of pleasure bereft of pain, sadness and misery. Suffering is the tool with which we fashion the spirit and thus cultivate character and personality. It is only now that I am able to look back over my life and pinpoint exactly when angels have helped me. I have always prayed and will continue to pray for continued help and guidance. Although they see exactly what is in our hearts and souls, our prayers form the ultimate acknowledgement that we know they are there, and to the Kingdom of Angels, this is of paramount importance.

Even though we mostly have free will and may therefore make our own decisions and reach our own conclusions, in many ways we are manipulated like marionettes, and what we believe has been our own decision in reality has not. Angels inspire and guide us all through our lives, and it is only when we have lost the fight through no fault of our own that they intervene, and then miracles thus occur. An atheist once declared that 'God does not exist, but angels most certainly do.' Even though the atheist had always dismissed the very existence of a Supreme Power, he admitted to having been helped by Angels.

All religions possess their archetypal angelic figures to which prayers are offered for help and guidance. So, if angels do not really exist, from where in our consciousness do they originate?

PENNIES FROM HEAVEN
Although there is a general consensus of opinion that one should never pray for money, occasionally some divine intervention comes about and pennies do seem to drop from heaven.

Some years ago now, I found myself in serious financial difficulty. I was driving by the cemetery on the far side of Wavertree Park, (the Mystery as it was known,) when I remembered that my paternal grandmother was in fact buried there. As a child I used to visit the grave regularly with my parents, but hadn't been to it for many years. I felt overwhelmed with the desire to see it again and thought it would be a good idea to stop and have a look at it.

I must say, I was extremely upset to see the state of my Gran's grave, and immediately set about tidying it up. It was obvious that nobody had visited the grave since my father had passed away in 1970. Although I hadn't known my father's mother, she had died when I was very small, I found her constantly in my mind for weeks after my visit to her grave.

About three months later, my brother, Alby, phoned me. 'Are you sitting down?' he asked, in a serious voice. 'If you're not, I suggest you do!'

I had no idea what he was talking about, but thought it must be something quite serious. My heart began to beat quickly and I did sit down to listen to what he had to say.

'Dad's sister has died,' he began excitedly, 'and it couldn't have come at a better time for us both.'

I still had no idea what my brother was talking about. Dad's sister, Louise, had lived in the family home till the day she died. Because of a family dispute after my grandmother's death, my Dad had not spoken to his sister for many years. She had become a recluse and was a little bit detached from reality, mentally speaking. 'She didn't leave a will.' He announced joyfully.

I still couldn't see why he was so excited, and then he told me why this was to our advantage. 'Her estate reverts back to the original will of our Grandfather.' He blurted. 'This means we get dad's share.'

I couldn't believe it. 'How much will we get?' I asked eagerly. I desperately needed the money to pay off all my debts. 'Come on, Alby, don't keep me in suspense.'

'Not sure,' he replied. 'There's the house in Penny Lane and some money in the bank.'

As it turned out the entire estate consisted of nine thousand pounds in the bank, and the double fronted house in the now famous Penny Lane. The house had to be sold, and the money divided between my father's brother, George, and my brother, Alby and myself. It took nearly a year for the house to be sold, but at least with my share I was able to discharge all my debts. When I tell this story I refer to it as Pennies from Heaven, because to me, that's exactly what it was. I've no doubt that angels were watching over me when I was tidying my grandmother's grave, and they came to my rescue once again.

CHAPTER TWENTY-EIGHT
MEDIUMSHIP AND THE
SCIENTIFIC FACTS

I have always said the one and most effective way to ascertain whether or not a medium is genuine would be to subject him or her to a polygraph apparatus (Lie detector) test to settle the question once and for all. The only problem is the majority of the not so genuine mediums believe so much in what they do that even the lie detector would fail to achieve positive results. In 1903 the whole subject fascinated Professor Tutinsky of Moscow University so much that he devoted several years of research in an endeavour to find out why some people had paranormal experiences and others did not. Unable to obtain university funding, with great personal sacrifice, Professor Tutinsky financed the whole project himself. Although Tutinsky's peers ridiculed the respected scientist, nothing could deter him from what eventually became his life's mission. Tutinsky's research led him to make a detailed analysis of the pineal gland, the walnut shaped gland deep within the brain. Although at that time very little was known about the function of the pineal gland, he found that it was considerably larger in a child than it was in an adult, and marginally more developed in a female than it was in a male. The notable professor was certain that the pineal gland was responsible for all of the brain's paranormal experience, and although he took great pains to avoid the word 'psychic,' his final conclusions forced him to accept that during paranormal experience the brain was in fact accessing a 'field' of activity beyond the parameters of traditional science. Further experiments revealed that the pineal gland radiated electro-magnetic waves, and these either increased or decreased according to the level of paranormal experience. By the end of his study Tutinsky was certain that the pineal gland was the very reason why children are more receptive to unseen forces than adults, and why women are far more sensitive to them than men.

Modern day research more or less agrees with Professor Tutinsky's scientific conclusions that mediums are not normal regardless of what spiritualists say about mediumistic skills. Upon examination the brain of a medium appears abnormally organised, and when he or she is actually working psychically there is some interruption to the neurological electrical circuitry. Some years ago now I volunteered to take part in some neurological experiments in which I was connected to an EEG (Electroencephalograph) and a bio-feedback apparatus. As well as the expected oscillation registering on the bio-feedback, the EEG showed significant changes in brain function, particularly when I was actually using my psychic skills. The EEG graph was quite erratic in places showing an obvious fluctuation in brain pattern. Although in my case the experiments were really not conclusive, they did however show the doctors conducting the experiments that 'something' was going on when I was psychically active. What exactly that was the psychiatrists and psychologists were not quite sure. The whole day's experiments left them completely mystified and very much in the dark regarding psychic skills. One doctor even suggested that I may be suffering from temporal lobe epilepsy and that this most probably was causing me to have some sort of mystical experience. Quite recently scientists have concluded that Saint Paul was an epileptic and that this condition was the very reason why he experienced the blinding light on the road to Damascus. In fact, the same scientific experiments concluded that people with temporal lobe epilepsy do have 'psychic' or 'spiritual' experiences when having an epileptic 'fit.' Scientists have also announced that they have isolated the module in the brain in which God or God-Consciousness exists. The mind boggles!

WHEN IS A HAUNTED HOUSE NOT A HAUNTED HOUSE

To a layman I suppose the appearance of a ghostly form constitutes a 'haunted' location. However, to a parapsychologist it is simply evidence of some form of metaphysical activity. The majority of hauntings are produced by an impregnation of energy in the psychic structure, a sort of a photographic image in the subtle atmosphere of the location. Should someone have died in tragic or traumatic circumstances, the very event causes energy to be discharged into the atmosphere, creating a permanent memory in the psychic structure of the area. This memory image is occasionally activated and a replay of the past emotional event manifests as a ghostly display. Of course, what is seen is only a metaphysical memory, and is not the actual spirit itself.

Another significant cause for paranormal activity may be the result of a geological phenomenon called Triboluminescence – friction caused by two quartz particles or similar substances below ground level. Such geological movement somehow affects molecular changes in the surrounding environment, and these changes may precipitate significant brain activity in some people, sufficiently enough to cause hallucinations. Those suffering from temporal lobe epilepsy are particularly susceptible to this phenomenon, and in these cases the hallucinations will persist as long as the sufferer remains within the confines of that location. We cannot exclude, of course, the possibility that a location is actually haunted by the spirit of a so-called 'dead' person, who simply refuses to move on. When it is a genuine haunting the ghostly apparition nearly always 'sees' the haunted location as it was when he or she actually lived there, and very rarely as it is now. This means then that although so-called 'ghosts' appear to see those who witness them, they do not. However, there are occasions when a spirit not only gives the impression that he or she can see you, but they then surprise you by talking.

CHAPTER TWENTY-NINE
MISCELLANEOUS
INFORMATION
INSPIRED BY THE SPIRIT

Over the years I have come to realise that my mediumistic abilities are frequently used as a conduit for inspirational ideas, of one kind or another. Even as a child I would frequently be seen staring into space, completely oblivious to my mother calling my name. Although everyone thought I was just daydreaming, as children do, I now know that this was my way of focusing my attention on the unseen areas of the supersensual world, where I watched unusual shapes and shadowy figures dancing in the air. I can recall a time when I was five years old, and my mother was concerned about the trouble I was having with my sinuses. I was doing my usual thing and staring into space, and only half aware of her expressing her concern to her friend. Suddenly, I blurted, 'They're telling me to tell you to get eucalyptus oil, mixed with Vaseline and a little warm water.' She just looked at me quizzically, and then turned to her friend and smiled. I'd no idea what eucalyptus was, and couldn't explain to my mother who 'they' actually were. At that point in my life all I knew was that things just seemed to come into my head, rather like a beam of light shining from above. I know this will sound a little far-fetched to a sceptic, and also to anyone who has never had a spiritual experience of any kind. But, the truth is mediumistic skills in children are very disconcerting, particularly to the children who experience them. Although my mother understood perfectly well exactly what was happening to me, I know that she thought I was an 'odd' little boy, and secretly prayed that I would grow out of it. I didn't, of course, and my skills eventually took control of my life, instead of me taking control of my psychic skills, as I do today.

In the early years of my work I felt so close to Tall Pine that it was almost as though he had stepped inside my body and taken over my mind. I would be completely oblivious to anything, and would just be aware of an overwhelming sense of peace and serenity. Although people always assumed that I was in a deep trance-like state, I do believe that I was just 'overshadowed' by Tall Pine, even though I was not aware of the philosophy I was expounding. Many years had gone by before I realised that Tall Pine was simply a 'Gate Keeper', and that the controlling spirit entity was a Victorian writer/philosopher, and one member of the group I now know as the Elders. Although I have no concrete proof, I am fairly certain that the discarnate personality who spoke through me was Belgium writer and mystic, Maurice Maeterlink, who in fact died on May 6th 1949, three years after I was born. There are far too many similarities between his writings and the philosophical discourses I used to expound, and when I eventually acquired a photograph of Maeterlink, I immediately felt I was looking at an old friend.

PRAYER

I have always believed that the need to pray is an essential part of our being, and although prayer itself can take many different forms, it is my opinion that believing in God is not a prerequisite for prayer. To me, prayer is the deepest form of meditation, and may be used as a powerful affirmation to connect the consciousness with the Universal Mind. Prayer may be used as a universal mantra, and instead of using it to humbly ask for Divine Help, it should be sent out into the universe with force and determination, instructing the universe to empower our souls, so that our dreams, wishes and desires may be gratified. Needless to say, the laws of the universe are always in constant operation, and should our prayers be selfish or designed to harm others, then we need to be prepared to take the consequences of our actions. Curses and Blessing truly do come home to roost. This is a law that is both right and just.

PRECOGNITION

We need first of all to define 'precognition' and the precognitive experience. I suppose that precognition can be very loosely described as 'overwhelming feelings of things that are going to happen!' Most people have had precognitive visions of one kind or another, and although these are usually dismissed as having no great significance, precognition is, itself, a psychic skill, and one that should never be underestimated. However, research has shown that the majority of precognitive visions are of doom and gloom disasters, and very rarely produce glimpses of anything joyous and uplifting. Why this is nobody quite knows. Precognition can also come in dreams. One example is of a woman who frequently had precognitive dreams, and was delighted to wake up one morning having dreamt of the brother she hadn't seen for twenty years returning home from Australia. He did return, just as in her dream, but was killed in a car accident on his way from the airport.

DRUG ADDICTS AFTER DEATH

During that horrible period of my life I found myself a sort of epicentre for those who had died tragically through drugs. My mediumistic skills had somehow made me into a 'rescue beacon' for those who were in distress in the spirit world and therefore needed some help and direction. Although I had empathy for those who had died as a consequence of drug abuse, I most certainly was not psychologically strong enough to offer the help they so badly needed to move them into the light. When a drug addict or alcoholic dies their addiction and craving does not magically disappear. For a short while their addiction causes them to remain in the lower vibratory spheres closest to the physical world, where they can continue to gratify their cravings and desires. Although they no longer have access to the substances they so badly need to satisfy their addictions, they are, however, able to influence and feed off the minds of those still alive in the physical world. The whole psychological process of a drug addict after death is completely out of his or her control. Their craving and addiction prevents them from accepting the fact that he or she has died. However, their sojourn in this state is transitory, and eventually all psychological ties to the physical world dissipate completely, and the soul is then drawn towards the light.

Mediums are beacons of light and must always be prepared for all eventualities. Because I had been in that psychological state I seemed to attract those in distress. Unfortunately, however, such distressed souls did not always seek help and guidance, but more to influence me to imbibe more and more narcotic substances. Only in this way could their craving and needs be gratified.

For me personally it has been a long and difficult journey, and one that I have had to travel alone. When I was at my lowest point in life I had no friends at all and frequently wandered around the streets of Liverpool alone and extremely depressed. I learnt my greatest lesson from those extremely hard and very difficult days, and that was not to place my trust in anyone at all. I once told an elderly man, 'All my friends have gone!'

'No,' He retorted. 'Your friends haven't gone. They were not your friends.'

And it is true, your friends never desert you. Had I not believed that angels were guiding me, I have no idea what I would have done. At that time in my life they were all the friends I really and truly had.

WHERE IS THE SPIRIT WORLD

The question that most people ask is, 'Where is the Spirit World?' And what the majority of people find difficult to understand is that the Spirit World is not a place. In fact, it has nothing whatsoever to do with places, and has no particular geographical location in the universe of earth, sky and human habitations. I suppose it would be more correct to say that the Spirit World is more a condition or state of being, rather than it is a place we go to when we die. We actually live in a multidimensional universe in which there are worlds within worlds, each rising in a gradually ascending vibratory scale, from those which touch and blend with the highest planes of the physical world, to those which gradually merge with the lowest realms of the Spirit World. However, although when we die we no longer inhabit a physical body, we do, to all intents and purposes, take on a replicated image of our former physical self. Whether one chooses to call this form an Astral Body, or a Spirit Body is of no great importance. The truth is, our essence lives on even after our physical body has disintegrated and has been resolved back into its original elements. It is said that the finite mind cannot comprehend the infinite, and the experience we have when we leave the physical body is purely transcendental, so therefore beyond human understanding. However, it is an axiom of physics that no two bodies of matter can occupy the same space at the same time; but literally millions upon millions of vibrations can exist in the same space without interference. And so, the Spirit World interpenetrates the physical world, and orbits within and around the physical atom. The so-called 'dead' are walking through and around us all the time, unaware of our presence just as the majority of us are completely unaware of them. The Spirit World is quite surreal, and possesses an extremely abstract landscape like nothing we in this world can imagine. There are no alternating periods of night and day, and time in the Spirit World is measured in a completely different way to that which we know in this world. The inhabitants of the spirit world are primarily governed by habit and conscience combined, and the only reward for achievements is the experience attained through the actual acts themselves. The Spirit World is in fact sub-divided into innumerable worlds, each one composed of a much finer substance than the one below it. And so, as I have already said, we live in a multidimensional universe, in which there are worlds within worlds, each rising in a gradually ascending vibratory scale.

CHAPTER THIRTY
THE HUMOUR AND THE
SADNESS OF MESSAGES

Demonstrating mediumistic skills on a theatre stage is completely different to demonstrating in the cosy environment of a Spiritualist Church. For one thing, a theatre audience pay for their tickets and so expect the medium to produce something. Besides, not all those who attend a theatre show know what to expect, and can very often be quite cruel if they don't receive a message. Although I never remember individual messages, the following examples have been taken from recordings that were done at my shows over the years, and which should give you a good idea of the different kinds of communications that mediums receive. In fact, some messages are quite funny, often proving that we still retain our sense of humour when we pass over.

On entering the spirit world there is no dramatic change in a person's personality – wings do not sprout and haloes do not suddenly appear. In the spirit world you become what you are; and what you have thought and felt in this life is what you will become in the next life. You cannot hide from your true self, and your conscience becomes your greatest judge. So Uncle Joe with the amazing sense of humour will return to say hello to you as 'Uncle Joe with the sense of humour'. It will take time for the irritable and bad tempered neighbour to become anything other than irritable and bad tempered! And that is how you will recognize him, should he communicate through a medium.

In a theatre one evening I spoke to an elderly lady on the front row.

'Your husband Sam is here,' I said and the lady began to

cry.

The microphone was taken to her so she could respond to the message and everyone now heard her say, 'Oh, Sam, dear Sam. He only died three weeks ago.'

'He wants you to know that he's fine,' I said. 'He's with Molly.'

'That's his sister!' the lady wailed down the microphone and started snuffling loudly into her handkerchief. 'He was close to her.'

Then, I heard Sam from the spirit world say loud and clear, 'Oh for God's sake, tell her to shut up! Tell her to stop whingeing! She never cared for me while I was here – she made my life a misery! She was a cow. The only reason I've taken the trouble to come to speak to her is to tell her that I am now with my first wife, Ann. I won't be waiting for her when she comes over.'

I looked down at the distraught woman who was being consoled by her friend, and I said, 'Sam is saying he loves you very much.' And I tried desperately not to laugh.

'What?' Sam shouted inside my head. 'Love that cow?' and he faded away, back into the spirit world, to be replaced, luckily, by communicators who did care for the lady!

Not a frequent occurrence, but one I shall never forget.

TELL LAURA I LOVE HER

On one theatre show in Essex, I had just begun my demonstration when a lady communicated with me from the Spirit World. She told me she desperately wanted to pass on a message to her daughter, Laura. The lady communicator felt quite weak, and she explained that she had only passed over a couple of weeks before. I wandered up and down the stage hoping that she would tell me exactly where her daughter was sitting, but unfortunately she left me to do all the work. 'I am looking for someone called Laura whose mother has only recently died,' I said nervously. The audience just stared blankly at me, as I moved uncomfortably around the open stage. I seemed to be getting no help whatsoever from the communicator, until she spoke to me again. 'Her name is Ratterson.' The spirit communicator blurted. I repeated this name to the audience, and almost immediately a young woman raised her hand. 'Your name is Ratterson?' I asked excitedly, relieved that the message was now beginning to take shape.

'That's my aunt's best friend's name,' she responded 'she passed away not so long ago.'

Then the lady communicator told me she had lived in Belgium, and that her husband was Flemish. I passed this information onto the young woman, and she confirmed that this was true.

'Then I have your mother here,' I announced. 'You must be Laura?'

'The young woman laughed. 'My mother's still alive. Laura is my sister.'

Her response threw me and I felt myself becoming more and more nervous. 'Tell Laura I love her,' the lady communicator continued. 'She is my daughter.'

At that point I didn't know what to say. 'You say that Laura is your sister?' I continued clumsily, my voice obviously revealing my nervousness.

'Correct,' she replied. 'Then I must have got this all wrong.' I confessed. 'This lady tells me she is Laura's mother, and that Laura's name is Ratterson.'

By now the young woman was becoming quite embarrassed, and was doing all that she could to help me. I could see that I was going round in circles, and so I made an excuse to terminate the message, and quickly went on to somebody else.

I must say the Lady communicator was with me for some time, and during the interval I could still feel her overwhelming presence. I was quite depressed and did not feel like going on with the show.

Some weeks later I received a long letter that had come to me via the theatre. It was from the young woman I had tried to give the message to. She had spoken to her mother who had eventually explained that her sister Laura was in fact adopted, and that her real mother had been the best friend of the young woman's aunt. Her name had in fact been Ratterson. Although the audience had been left thinking I had made a mess of the whole message, at least I had learned the truth and now knew that my message was correct.

Demonstrating mediumistic skills in theatres is not like an actor learning his or her lines in a play. On the contrary, a medium has no idea what is going to happen when he or she walks out onto the stage. The whole process involves a great deal of skill and hard work, as well as faith and cooperation from the spirit world. No medium can guarantee results, simply because we just do not know what is going to happen.

CHAPTER THIRTY-ONE
THE GHOSTS OF THE
DEE ESTUARY

Four years ago my wife, Dolly and I, rented a farmhouse in Lower Heswall, over looking the very picturesque Dee Estuary. Waking up in the morning to such a beautiful view was so invigorating and made so much difference to each day that we never wanted to move. There had been a dwelling house on the farm since the twelfth century and the whole area was steeped in history, from the invasion of the Vikings to the occupation of the Romans. From our window we could see the Welsh Hills across the Estuary, and even an approaching storm would look breathtaking as it moved menacingly across the water towards us like a dark cloud of locusts moving in to devour everything in its path. In fact, living on the farm was an inspiration to me and we both loved just being there. Just watching the sun set on the estuary was a sight to behold, and then the morning sounds of birdsong and the cacophony of cows and hens waking to the day made the whole thing just perfect. However, when darkness descended it always seemed to me as though a command had been given for all the creatures of the farm to lay their sleepy heads and be silent, and apart from the occasional hoot of an owl from its nearby watching place, everything was stilled beneath the dark mantel of eerie silence.

We'd been living there for five months and already spooky things had begun to happen. Strange luminous mists would move slowly about the bedroom, and disembodied whispers would echo through the night. Although I am used to such spooky goings on, I must admit that I was beginning to feel unnerved by all the phenomena that seemed to be completely out of my control.

There was a sandstone wall and cobbles all around the house, and even the slightest movement outside would resound through the empty spaces across the farm. It was late October and the moon was hiding behind misty clouds as the hypnotic sound of the old clock in the bedroom carefully marked out each second to the hour of 1am. I was lying there unable to sleep, my mind playing over the events of the day and the things I had to do in the morning, when I heard footsteps on the cobbles outside. I woke Dolly and together we peered nervously through the bedroom window into the darkness. By then the moon was peeping slyly from behind the misty clouds, its ghostly light dissipating the shadows across the cobbled courtyard. We gasped as we caught sight of five hooded shadowy figures walking slowly across the courtyard, their ghostly forms silhouetted by the light of the moon as they moved purposefully off into the darkness. We waited at the window to see the shadowy forms return ten minutes later to make their way back towards the Estuary. This time we could see that they were attired in the robes of monks and were all extremely tall and walked with their heads bowed. The following night we saw them again, and watched with intrigue as the ghostly monastic figures followed the same route across the cobbled courtyard and then returned ten minutes later to make their way back towards the estuary from whence they came. In fact, we saw the ghostly shadowy forms every night for the following two weeks, and so decided to take a closer look. On the Friday night we took a duvet and some pillows out to the car and then made ourselves comfortable ready for our ghostly encounter. To make the evening more enjoyable we took a bottle of Veuve Clicquot Champagne, two glasses and armed ourselves with the appropriate paranormal equipment, an EMF meter (Electro-Magnetic Frequency) a non-contact thermometer with a laser and a night vision camera. We were all set and waited patiently for the haunting hour to approach. We sipped our Champagne and glared through the car window into the darkness nervously waiting for our ghostly friends to arrive. Unfortunately that's all we remember. We both woke up about 4am shivering with the cold and me having spilled a glass of Champagne all over my shirt. We were absolutely freezing and missed the whole spooky scenario. The following day we laughed at the thought of the ghostly monastic figures peering at us through the car window, bewildered and wondering exactly why we were asleep in the car.

Being a medium can sometimes be a lot of fun, providing you do not take things too seriously.

CHAPTER THIRTY-TWO
MORE PSYCHIC
EXPERIENCES FROM
MY PAST

When I now look back over my life, I am frequently overwhelmed with many regrets. Although somewhat of a cliché, they do say that hindsight is a wonderful thing. However, to be quite honest, if I could turn back the clock I really wouldn't change one single thing. I may have done things slightly different, but I would still have walked exactly the same path as I did. I must say though, in comparison to teenagers today I was extremely immature and very selfish. My psychic skills had never left me, but overloaded with the energies of a teenager, all I wanted to do was be a musician, have lots of girls and become wealthy. I wasn't really bothered which came first, as long as all my dreams were eventually fulfilled.

A psychically inclined person is expected to have many paranormal experiences, and I was certainly no exception. I purposely left these stories until this point in the book, as along with the Lady of Light episode in my younger life, these were most probably some of the most significant paranormal events in my adult life.

THE DISAPPEARING STABLE
Sometime in the mid sixties I felt as though I had had enough of touring with my band. I decided to take off for a few days break with some friends without telling my fellow band members, but when our money ran out we began to make our way back home. We were hitching a lift through

Wales and found ourselves stranded late at night in Prestatyn, North Wales, with nowhere to sleep. I asked a guy on his way home from a night out at the pub if he knew of any hotels or boarding houses in the area, and as it was so late he suggested that we spend the night with him. The only thing was he lived in a disused stable on the farm where he worked. We had no choice, and so we graciously accepted.

Although very sparse and only a blanket or two to sleep on, at least it was fairly warm and dry and a place to rest our heads until morning, and for this my friends and I were grateful. Our host also apologised for the mess, and said that there had been a fire there some weeks before, and this was the reason why everything was in such disarray. He then went on to explain that the stable was haunted and that in the early hours of the morning the sound of a chain could be heard beating against an extremely distressed horse. Our host was quite nonchalant about the whole ghostly tale, and then settled himself down to sleep.

Sure enough as he had said, we woke up around 3 am to the ghostly sounds of a distressed horse, rearing on its hind legs and neighing, as the clanking of a chain echoed eerily between the empty stable walls. The room we had been sleeping in was divided from the main part of the stable by a crudely constructed wooden partition. The three of us quickly went to investigate the ghostly sounds, only to witness old newspapers, straw and soil being thrown all over the place, and even though the cacophony of chilling disembodied sounds continued, the stable itself was absolutely empty. Although we hadn't noticed it then our host had gone. We looked everywhere to thank him for his hospitality, but he was nowhere to be found. Needless to say we didn't hang around very long and vacated the stable as quickly as we could.

Some weeks later I returned to Prestatyn with some friends, hoping to show them exactly where we encountered the ghostly commotion of the horse being beaten to death. To my great surprise the stable had gone, disappeared completely. I made a few enquiries in the village to be told that there hadn't been a stable there for many years, and that it had been destroyed in a fire forty years before. SPOOKY!

THE HAUNTED THEATRE

When I began working as a Stage Medium many years later, I was appearing at the Neptune theatre in the Liverpool City centre. My first autobiography had just been published and the Neptune theatre was a part of my book launch theatre tour. The tickets had sold out two weeks before the event, and we had arrived at the theatre a couple of hours before the show was due to start. I was wandering around at the back of the stage, nostalgically recalling when I had played there as a young musician many years before. My manager was at the front of the theatre talking to the box office attendant, and the back stage staff had not yet arrived. I made my way slowly down the stone steps towards the Green Room, somewhat intrigued that nothing whatsoever had changed in all those years. As I reached the bottom of the steps, a tall well-dressed gentleman walked passed me and smiled. Thinking that I was down there alone, the man naturally startled me. He obviously realised what he had done, and stopped at the foot of the steps and looked at me apologetically. 'I'm sorry,' he said in a deep voice. 'I was just checking everything was secure.' As my show was scheduled to begin at 8pm, I looked quizzically at the man who didn't seem to know why I was there. He shrugged and, turning away from me, began to ascend the steps. I looked away from him for a brief moment, and when I looked up the steps he was nowhere to be seen. I felt a chill pass over me, and I quickly ran to the top of the steps to see where he had gone, but he was nowhere in sight. In fact, there was no one back stage, and nobody knew who the man was. I later discovered

170

that the gentleman I had encountered by the Green Room, was in actually fact one of the original owners of the theatre - a Mr Crane. He was one of the Crane brothers, and had hanged himself in the theatre many years before. On another visit to the theatre, one of the staff told me that Mr Crane is frequently seen in the Green Room, and that some of the staff had actually seen his reflection in the mirror, grinning mischievously at them. Needless to say, I have never set foot in the Green Room ever again.

CHAPTER THIRTY-THREE
THE MORE HUMOROUS
SIDE OF MY WORK

AN INVITATION I NEARLY COULDN'T REFUSE

Another absolutely hilarious event in my life took place some years later when I started the Thought Workshop. In the early days our meetings were actually held in the Liberal centre above a hairdresser's shop on Smithdown Road. We met there every Thursday evening and there would be a different subject covered each week. Our meetings were always full to capacity, and as well as our loyal supporters, each week would always bring along someone new. One particular night a young woman wandered through the door clutching two small packages. She asked if she could have a word with me, and I explained that it would be more convenient to talk at the end of the evening. And so, when the lecture had finished and the majority of people had left, I sat down with the young woman to listen to what she had to say. First of all she showed me some intricate sketches of geometric shapes, and explained to me that they had been channelled through her by some 'higher minds' and that they had instructed her to find me. I was intrigued to know more, and sat back and listened. 'I am a part of group very similar to the one you run,' she began, but the object of our meetings is to create healing energy and transmit it to poverty stricken nations.' I thought it was quite fascinating, but wanted to know how I could help. 'We create the healing energy by sexually interacting with each other.' I could feel my mouth drop open and I sat forward. 'We would like you to join?' I was somewhat taken aback and couldn't speak for a few moments. 'This book explains the nature of our work.'

She proffered a brown envelope containing the mysterious book. I declined to take it.

'Erm!' I stuttered uncomfortably. 'I … I am far too busy with my work.' I made a clumsy excuse, and then one of my colleagues joined us. As well as being quite curious, he was also extremely naïve and was obviously very interested in the attractive young woman.

No more was said and the woman left.

The summer was hot and our meeting place was sweltering. My colleague was late for the Thursday evening meeting and arrived when we were already half an hour into the lecture. He looked rather dishevelled and very flustered. I saw that he was clutching the young woman's book in his hands. I couldn't help but smile. He had obviously been pulled into the strange group – any excuse!

He later told me that she had taken him for a drive into the countryside of Wales. It had been a beautiful day and they had meditated together in a field, with only the sweet smell of honeysuckle and monotonous drone of the bee. Having put a daisy chain around his head, the next thing he knew he was dancing with her naked around a tree, completely oblivious to anything other than the peaceful sounds of summer. Suddenly, there was a distant cacophony of singing, bringing him with a jolt back to reality. He looked over to the gate and saw a group of small cubs with their Akela, all staring with amazement at him and his nude companion. Their clothes were resting on the grass over by the gate, and so covering themselves as best as they could, they quickly recovered their things and then made a hasty retreat. 'What have I got myself involved with?' he moaned. 'I can't believe it. I thought she was genuinely after my mind'.

I just laughed. 'I can believe it,' I said sarcastically shaking my head. 'Any excuse!'

LOST TIME AND THE MYSTERIOUS WATCH

Each week we would cover a different topic. One week there would be a lecture or workshop, and the next week a demonstration of clairvoyance. Mavis Mitchell was a visually handicapped medium, and perhaps one of the best mediums in the northwest of England. I had known Mavis for a very long time, and would always play jokes on her. However, she always took it in good fun and would very often get me back somehow. I had invited her to an evening of Psychometry, something Mavis really had an aptitude for, and would always amaze the audience with the accuracy of her messages. This night we invited the audience to place personal items on a tray that one of my colleagues took around. There were over fifty people present that night and the tray was full of rings, brooches, bracelets and many watches. As always Mavis went right into her demonstrations and began giving each person a small but very precise message from the articles she had selected from the tray. She never liked to disappoint anyone, and so she was always determined to give everyone a message. Although our meetings normally finished around 9.30 prompt, when Mavis Mitchell was on we never finished any earlier than 11.30, and even then she would stay behind to talk to some of the audience. This night everything went well. She had given everyone a message and returned their items of jewellery to each person. The remaining item on the tray was an old lady's watch. Mavis held the item in her hands and proceeded to relate the information. 'Is that correct?' she called out. But there was no response. 'Hello,' she joked. Whose watch is this?' Everyone in the audience looked curiously around, but there was still no response. The evening ended, and after thanking Mavis Mitchell, everyone left. We, however, were baffled as we carefully examined the mysterious watch that nobody ever claimed. I still have the watch to this very day. Although Mavis sadly passed away in her sleep a few years ago, I frequently feel her presence.

The popularity of mediums on television today has given rise to an increase in the amount of so-called clairvoyants and mediums working in theatres all over the UK. The lack of a governing body means that anyone is free to begin working as a medium, and as a result the theatre circuit is absolutely saturated with them. Solely depending on exactly what your idea of a 'genuine' medium is, it might be very difficult to understand that because a medium is well known and working in the public eye, does not necessarily mean he or she is genuine. However, even before mediums ever appeared on television, charlatans have been an integral part of Spiritualism. Eddy Emmery, (previously mentioned elsewhere), related these stories to me not long before he passed away sometime in the 1980s.

Eddy attended a physical circle in Liverpool for some years in the late 1950s. Because of the nature of the circle, the séance room was always kept locked until ten minutes before the séance was to commence. As arranged, everyone would always arrive forty minutes before to have the obligatory pre-séance cup of tea and a chat, primarily to get the 'vibes' right and put everyone in the 'mood'. The séance was actually conducted at the home of the medium in control of it, and he had been a friend of Eddy Emmery's for many years. There had never previously been any doubt in Eddy's mind that his friend was genuine, and although the medium had never been one for seeking recognition or fame for his skill as a physical medium, Eddy Emmery's growing suspicion took hold of him. The fact that the séance room had to be kept clean and in total darkness had always been an accepted part of the loyal circle's principles, but there were other annoying things that constantly came into Eddy's mind. He was not happy and wanted so much to prove to himself that the phenomena produced in his friend's séance room was genuinely from the spirit world. Although Eddy had always loved his Friday night sojourn in the séance room, he so badly needed to know if his friend was not pulling the wool over everyone's eyes. Eddy knew that the séance room door was always unlocked fifteen minutes before everyone went upstairs where the room was situated at the top of the house. Whilst everyone was finishing their cups of tea, Eddy made his excuses to visit the bathroom and then discretely snuck upstairs unnoticed. As he expected the séance room door was unlocked. Eddy crept in and carefully inspected the mediums ornately calved chair. Each week apports would drop through the darkened room onto the laps of selected members of the séance circle, and the lucky recipients would take home their treasured artefacts of rings, earrings, brooches and anything the spirit world chose to give. Eddy had been curious for some time, and now he had the opportunity to inspect the chair upon which his friend would fall into a deep trance each week. To his horror he discovered a concealed drawer under the seat of the chair, in which there were the alleged apports for the séance. Eddy was disgusted and overwhelmed with a feeling of being totally let down by his friend. After removing all the artefacts, he replaced them with a quantity of jelly babies he had in his pocket. To everyone's great surprise each person in the séance received a jelly baby. Well done Eddy Emmery!

GABRIEL'S TRUMPET

Another veteran medium (now deceased) also sat for many years in a circle in which disembodied voices would speak through a trumpet. The medium supervising the séance attributed the weekly phenomena to his spirit guide, known to him as 'Gabriel'. John Sadler always looked forward to his weekly meeting, and although he never failed to be enthralled when the trumpet whirled quickly round the circle, it also gave him the opportunity to say a few words. However, as John Sadler was only a guest in the small group, he would always politely wait until the supervising medium had done his thing, and the disembodied voice had spoken. The Monday night séance went as planned, and John waited patiently until the last voice had resounded through the aluminium trumpet before he stood up to speak. John himself also spoke whilst in a semiconscious trance state and, as he was never aware of what he had said he relied on others to tell him. However, this night whilst John was still speaking in the blacked out room, the trumpet began to whirl around again in front of him, spilling out the mumblings of disembodied voices. Unaware of this, John concluded his oratory and, still disorientated, stepped back to lower himself onto his chair. Instead, though, he stumbled over something and fell heavily back, cracking his head on the corner of a huge Victorian sideboard and knocking himself unconscious. Hearing the commotion, a lady sitter quickly turned on the lights to see that John had stumbled over the supervising medium, who had been on his hands and knees moving the trumpet around the circle. The medium had been faking the phenomena for years and thanks to John Sadler, Gabriel and his horn was banished from the séance room forever.

Unfortunately, as this sort of phenomena requires total darkness, it leaves itself wide open to fakery and charlatanism. Sad, but that's how it is and probably always will be!

CHAPTER THIRTY-FOUR
THE PARANORMAL CRAZE

I have no doubt in my mind that there is a paranormal craze sweeping the world at the moment. Primarily because of the numerous television programmes being broadcast on Sky television interest in mediums and the paranormal has increased and new terminology has evolved and become fashionable amongst the devotees of these programmes. In fact, because of television programmes like 'Most Haunted, Ghost Towns', and 'Dead Famous', to name but a few, it has become quite 'trendy' to be involved in the paranormal, and any commonplace sound or light reflection is now nearly always misconstrued as 'paranormal activity' or 'Spirit Light anomaly'. Terms such as 'Residual energy', 'grounded' and 'in visitation' are fast becoming integral parts of new dialogue used completely out of context by television paranormal investigators and celebrity mediums. Because of the growing popularity of these paranormal programmes it would seem that everyone in the general public has become privy to this new wave of terminology. My office at the Paranormal Study Centre receives at least twenty phone calls a day, each one a request for help concerning movement of furniture, sounds, strange lights and things going bump in the night. It all sounds quite intriguing until I hear the person on the other end of the phone coming out with that all too familiar jargon, which immediately tells me they are devotees of one of these many ridiculous programmes. 'I am not too sure whether or not it's just residual,' the person may say, 'I saw an orb' and then 'it's grounded not in visitation'. When I ask, 'Do you watch Most Haunted?' There is usually a pause, before the answer, 'Yes,' sharply comes. 'But how do you know?' Is usually what follows.

'Just a guess!' I normally say politely, desperately holding back what I really want to say, 'interesting programme!'

Although a lot of these programmes have opened up the minds of the general public to the paranormal and the way mediums work, they have also given a completely wrong impression. Having appeared on television all over the world, I know only too well just how a programme can be edited to make it more interesting and visually effective, often making the medium far better than what he or she actually is. An example of this was when I appeared on the popular Maltese television programme XARABANK. Having to demonstrate my mediumistic skills to an audience of two hundred Catholics for approximately five hours was quite daunting, to say the least. Although I worked extremely well during the evening, the programme was also edited to show the viewer exactly how editing could work against as well as for the medium. A clip of my demonstration was shown with all the positive information I had given, removed, so that it looked as though those who received messages were saying 'No' to everything I said. The programme was also edited to show a positive side of my demonstration, with all the people who received messages from me responding with a 'Yes', making me look exceptionally good. However, as I have already said in a previous chapter, my overall demonstration was quite evidential and did receive an overwhelming response from the entire audience.

The craze does not end with television programmes about the paranormal. There is a growing interest in psychic development and wanting to be a medium just like those on television. My office has a growing database of names and addresses of people wanting courses and workshops so that they can learn how to be a medium. The majority of those coming to the workshops quickly lose interest and abandon the idea when they see it's not really for them when they see there's more to it than they thought. However, a minority do persevere and go on to develop some semblance of psychic skill. Although many people cultivate their psychic skills primarily as a means of making easy money, unless they've got the strength and stamina they are usually greatly disappointed. Working as a psychic is extremely difficult and requires dedication, patience and determination.

THE FINAL CHAPTER
BUT NOT THE END

I have to say that from a very early age, for one reason or another, I have found life to be a huge challenge. For one thing, my health has always presented problems for me, and made it difficult for me to lead a normal life. Still, I somehow managed to cope, simply by creating my life around my debilitating illness, and have never allowed my illness to pull me completely down. Even so, I have enjoyed my life and would not have changed one single thing. My only regret is that I was not more successful in my career as a musician, and do wish I'd never turned down some of the opportunities that were offered to me in the 60s. Although I never used my health as an excuse for turning down some of the offers of contracts to work in the USA, I knew full well that the respiratory disease with which I had suffered all my life put me under constant threat and prevented me from leading the normal life that the others guys in the band were able to lead. Now that I'm older, my mortality seems to present much more of a problem, and follows me closely, rather like a ghostly shadow waiting to pounce. My work as a medium has somehow made me quite morbid and causes me to be frequently overcome by periods of deep depression. I am not sure whether my years of drug abuse have made me this way, or whether I would have been like this anyway.

TALL PINE HAS THE FINAL WORD – HIS THOUGHTS

'Your loved ones do not die; they merely move to a different place in your heart!'

'Nought is there upon man bestowed, which by the soul cannot be borne.'

'Life is a great marathon, but keep pace only with yourself and then you will always be the victor.'

'Faith is believing without seeing, feeling without touching, and being happy and complete within yourself without receiving.'

'The distance between war and peace is but a thought.'

'You cannot stroke an animal with one hand, and then pick its bones with the other. Animals do not live for your consumption, for like you they have souls.'

'Love is the only gift that should always be returned.'